Bringing the Reggio Approach to your Early Years Practice

This easy-to-read series provides an introduction to some of the most important early years philosophies and shows how they can be incorporated into your setting. Each book provides:

- An outline of the background to the approach

- Clear explanations of the relevance to contemporary thinking

- Suggestions to help you to plan a successful learning environment

- Examples of what the individual approach can look like in practice.

Have you ever wondered what the Reggio Approach is all about, why it works, and how it can be used to benefit the young children in your setting?

The book describes how educators in Reggio Emilia work with young children, and looks at the connections between the Reggio Approach and the principles and commitments of the revised Early Years Foundation Stage (EYFS) framework. It provides practical examples involving children of different ages in a wide variety of settings, helping the reader to see the connection between practice and theory.

This new edition has been fully updated to show the connections between the Reggio Approach and the principles and commitments of the recently revised EYFS framework. Each chapter focuses on one important aspect of the Reggio Approach and includes:

- Practical examples involving children of different ages in a wide variety of settings, helping the reader to see the connection between practice and theory

- Questions to enable the reader to reflect on and develop his or her own practice in accordance with new statutory requirements

- References to sources of further reading and information.

This convenient guide will help early years practitioners, students and parents to really understand what the Reggio Approach can offer their setting and children.

Linda Thornton has extensive experience in the field of education and childcare. She has provided consultancy and training for local authorities, children's centres, nurseries and schools across the UK.

Pat Brunton has provided training and consultancy for local authorities, children's centres, nurseries and schools across the UK.

Bringing the Reggio Approach to your Early Years Practice

THIRD EDITION

Linda Thornton and Pat Brunton
Series edited by Sandy Green

Routledge
Taylor & Francis Group

LONDON AND NEW YORK

Third edition published 2014
by Routledge
2 Park Square, Milton Park, Abingdon, Oxon OX14 4RN

and by Routledge
711 Third Avenue, New York, NY 10017

Routledge is an imprint of the Taylor & Francis Group, an informa business

British Library Cataloguing in Publication Data
A catalogue record for this book is available from the British Library

Library of Congress Cataloging in Publication Data
Thornton, Linda.
Bringing the Reggio approach to your early years practice / Linda Thornton, Pat Brunton. -- 3rd edition.
pages cm -- (Bringing... to your early years practice)
ISBN 978-0-415-72909-3 (hardback) -- ISBN 978-0-415-72912-3 (paperback) -- ISBN 978-1-315-81354-7 (e-book) 1. Education, Preschool--Philosophy. 2. Early childhood education--Philosophy. 3. Education, Preschool--Italy-- Reggio Emilia. 4. Reggio Emilia approach (Early childhood education)
I. Brunton, Pat. II. Title.
LB1140.3.T46 2014
372.21--dc23
2013035570

First edition published by Routledge 2007
Second edition published by Routledge 2010

ISBN: 978-0-415-72909-3 (hbk)
ISBN: 978-0-415-72912-3 (pbk)
ISBN: 978-1-315-81354-7 (ebk)

Typeset in Optima
by Saxon Graphics Ltd, Derby

MIX
Paper from
responsible sources
FSC
www.fsc.org   FSC® C013056

Printed and bound in Great Britain by
TJ International Ltd, Padstow, Cornwall

Contents

Acknowledgements

We are grateful to the parents, children and staff of these early years settings, schools and organisations for the use of the photographs in this book:

Bridgwater Children's Centre, Bridgwater, Somerset
Crossens Nursery School, Southport, Sefton
Dolphin Nursery, Bracknell and Tooting, London
Ilfracombe Children's Centre, Ilfracombe, Devon
Lescudjack Children's Centre, Penzance, Cornwall
Soundabout Early Years Arts Project, Penzance, Cornwall
St Breock Primary School, Wadebridge, Cornwall

The photos of the city of Reggio Emilia are the authors' own.

Introduction

A piazza in the centre of Reggio Emilia

The preschools and infant-toddler centres of Reggio Emilia in Northern Italy are recognised around the world as examples of high-quality, child-centred early years settings. Thousands of people have taken part in Study Tours to Reggio, visited the 'Hundred Languages of Children Exhibition' or attended training on what is called the Reggio Approach. There are now many settings in the United Kingdom which have introduced new ways of working after they have been inspired by what they have seen or heard.

It is important to understand that the Reggio Approach is not a system or a method. Instead, the Reggio Approach is a long-term educational research project, constantly evolving as educators reflect on their practical experience of young children's learning processes. In Reggio theory comes out of practice, rather than practice being determined by a fixed educational theory.

Educators in Reggio are happy to share their experience and understanding of working with young children, but they are quick to point out that you can't 'do Reggio'.

In the words of Amelia Gambetti of Reggio Children:

> No-one in Reggio wants to teach others how to 'do school'. ... What we want to do is to look together for the values we might have in common, in order to build a better tomorrow.
>
> (Gambetti 1998)

If we want to bring the influence of the Reggio Approach to our early years settings in the UK, we can begin by identifying the values which we share with colleagues in Reggio Emilia.

The principles of good early years practice in the UK

Good early years practice in the UK:

- is based on strong relationships between both children and adults and values the involvement of parents in their children's learning;

- involves reflective practitioners who value all children as individuals, provide a high-quality environment and understand the different ways in which children develop and learn;

- requires practitioners who plan extended time for creative and challenging activities based on children's interests and previous experiences.

The Early Years Foundation Stage (EYFS) framework seeks to provide:

- **quality and consistency** in all early years settings, so that every child makes good progress and no child gets left behind;

- **a secure foundation** through learning and development opportunities which are planned around the needs and interests of each individual child and are assessed and reviewed regularly;

- **partnership working** between practitioners and with parents and/or carers;

- **equality of opportunity** and anti-discriminatory practice, ensuring that every child is included and supported.

The framework is based on four guiding principles which should shape practice in early years settings:

- every child is a **unique child**, who is constantly learning and can be resilient, capable, confident and self-assured;

- children learn to be strong and independent through **positive relationships**;

- children learn and develop well in **enabling environments**, in which their experiences respond to their individual needs and there is a strong partnership between practitioners and parents and/or carers; and

- **children develop and learn in different ways and at different rates**.

The key values of the Reggio Approach

In Reggio the high-quality experiences provided for young children are built on a set of key values. These have been developed over many years to reflect what the community of Reggio Emilia feels is important for young children and their families.

The Reggio Approach values:

- a powerful image of the child – it views children as strong, confident and competent;

- relationships where children, 'teachers' and parents are all equally important;

- children's creativity – it emphasises the importance of the environment in supporting children's development, play and learning;

- understanding how children learn, as individuals and in groups – it does this through setting aside time for long-term projects and reflective practice.

Learning from the Reggio Approach

To understand how to bring inspiration from the Reggio Approach to your early years practice you need to know about all the different pieces of the jigsaw which fit together to make up the whole picture.

In Chapter 1 you will find background information to 'set the scene'. This explains the history of the Reggio Approach, what has influenced its development and how the infant-toddler centres and preschools are organised.

Chapters 2 to 7 then look in turn at one aspect of the Reggio Approach in more detail. Each chapter looks at:

- what happens in Reggio;

- connections to the revised EYFS framework;

- how we can draw inspiration from the Reggio Approach;

- a 'Snapshot' illustrating how the ideas might look in practice;

- suggestions for further reading and research;

- a list of 'Questions to think about' to help you and your colleagues reflect on your current practice and to plan any changes you may want to make.

Chapter 2 focuses on relationships – between adults and children, between early years practitioners and parents, and between early years settings and their local communities.

In Chapter 3 we look in more detail at creativity – the environment and resources which support creativity, the different ways in which young children express their creativity and the importance of managing 'risky freedom'.

The role of the environment is explored in Chapter 4 – how visibility, flexibility, light and shadow, reflection and multi-sensory spaces can be used to enhance young children's learning and development.

The management of time is the focus for Chapter 5 – making the most of opportunities for children to explore and investigate, communicate, think and reflect, eat and drink, sleep and rest, be outdoors and be involved in long-term projects.

Chapter 6 discusses learning and teaching – developing children's ideas and theories, planning open-ended projects, individual and group learning, documentation, sharing learning with parents and celebrating learning.

Finally, Chapter 7 looks at the importance of reflective practice – working as part of a team, sharing skills and expertise, valuing others' opinions, carrying out action research and taking responsibility for one's own professional development.

Reference

Gambetti, A. (1998) *ReChild 2*. Reggio Children.

Further reading

Not Just Anyplace (2003) Video. Reggio Children.

This video tells the story of the Reggio experience from its earliest beginnings in Villa Cella. The philosophy and pedagogy are described by educators working in Reggio, and there are some short video sequences filmed in the preschools and infant-toddler centres.

Background to the Reggio Approach

History

The Reggio Approach to early childhood has been developed in Reggio Emilia, a small city in northern Italy which places great importance on services for children and families.

The XXVth Aprile preschool in Villa Cella

Reggio Emilia is a prosperous city with a long tradition of banking, trade and manufacturing which goes back to Roman times. It is surrounded by rural areas which include many small farms and small-holdings. Reggio has always been an area where social responsibility is taken seriously and where everyone is expected to play a part in the life of the local community.

The earliest preschool was founded in 1945 at the end of the Second World War. This area of Italy was devastated by the effects of the war and many of the young men were killed. In the small village of Villa Cella, on the outskirts of Reggio Emilia, a small amount of money was given to the community following the sale of a tank, a few horses and an abandoned truck. The villagers had to begin to rebuild their lives and they decided that they would start by building a preschool. They saw this as a way of giving their children a better future by building a new type of school – one where children would be taken seriously and believed in.

In the 1960s the local council, or municipality, of Reggio Emilia took over responsibility for developing and managing a network of preschools, for children aged 3 to 6, which were committed to the Reggio Approach.

In 1970 the network was expanded when the first infant-toddler centre, for infants aged 3 months to 3 years, was opened. This was in response to the needs of mothers with younger children, who wanted to return to work.

In 1991 the American magazine, *Newsweek*, named the Diana preschool as one of the ten best schools in the world. This led to a lot of interest in the Reggio Approach from around the world. In 1994 the organisation Reggio Children was set up to manage this interest, and to organise international study tours.

Influences

The key person responsible for the development of the Reggio Approach was Loris Malaguzzi. In 1945 Loris Malaguzzi was a primary school teacher working in Reggio Emilia. When he heard about the preschool that was being built in Villa Cella he cycled to the village to find out what was happening. Listening to the women who were working, and discovering how important the preschool was to them, he was inspired to learn more about very young children by training as a psychologist. Until he died in 1994, Loris Malaguzzi dedicated his life to developing what we now call the Reggio Approach.

The way in which the Reggio Approach has developed has been influenced by the culture of the surrounding area. In their everyday lives, the people of Reggio Emilia enjoy meeting others, being involved in discussions and sharing different points of view. Change is not seen as something to be frightened of. Adults and children are open to new ideas and are happy to try different ways of doing things.

Under the guidance of Loris Malaguzzi, the staff of the infant-toddler centres and preschools in Reggio studied examples of good practice from around the world. In developing the Reggio Approach they have been influenced by the ideas of Maria Montessori and Jean Piaget's theories on thinking and language. Interest in Lev Vygotsky's research into the connection between social interaction and cognitive development has led to a focus on group learning. Influences have also come from a wide range of artists, scientists, writers, poets and thinkers, many of whom have preschools or infant-toddler centres in Reggio named after them, for example Paulo Freire, Michelangelo and Pablo Neruda.

The front of the Municipal Theatre in Reggio Emilia

The renowned American educationalists Jerome Bruner and Howard Gardner both have a keen interest in the work of the educators in Reggio. They are involved in ongoing research projects into increasing our understanding of how young children think and learn.

Organisation

There are now 78 preschools and infant-toddler centres in and around the city of Reggio Emilia.

Children attend infant-toddler centres and preschools regularly throughout the week. From the age of 3 a child normally attends full time, five days a week.

The standard day runs from 9.00 am to 3.30 pm and an extended day from 7.30 am to 6.20 pm is available for working parents.

Work shifts are organised so that all staff are present in the morning when the centres are busiest. Ratios of adults to children are very similar to those in the UK. Staffing rotas are planned so that staff can meet together regularly to share observations, information and ideas on a daily and weekly basis.

Staff roles

Some of the staff roles in the early childhood centres are very similar to those in the UK, and others are very different.

Teacher

In Reggio the word 'teacher' is used for the staff who work with the children in the same way as the term 'practitioner' is used in the UK. Teachers work in pairs. They plan together and support the children as they are playing and working together in groups.

Each pair of teachers usually stays with the same group of children from the time they start in the centre until they move on to either preschool or elementary school. This allows the teachers to establish strong relationships with the children and their families.

Atelierista

Each preschool and infant-toddler centre has an atelierista as a staff member. An atelierista has skills and interests in a range of creative forms of expression. He or she may be an artist, a musician, a dancer, a photographer, a geologist or an ICT expert. The atelierista works with the teachers to help them plan and carry out long-term projects with the children. They also share their creative skills with the children and staff.

Pedagogista

The municipal network of early childhood centres is coordinated by a team of pedagogistas. Each pedagogista has responsibility for a small group of infant-toddler centres and preschools. They organise work schedules, deliver staff training and meet with parents, as well as advising teachers on long-term projects and the learning environment.

The key values of the Reggio Approach

The next six chapters look in turn at each of the key values of the Reggio Approach. These are:

- Relationships
- Creativity
- The environment
- Time
- Learning and teaching
- Reflective practice.

Further reading

Barazzoni, R. (2000) *Brick by Brick. The History of the 'XXV Aprile' People's Nursery School of Villa Cella*. (English Edition). Italy: Reggio Children.

A description of the early days of the first preschool, started on Liberation Day in 1945, through to the present day. A description of the historical, political and social influences which have helped to shape the Reggio experience.

Baldini, R., Cavallini, I. and Vecchi, V. (2012) *One City, Many Children: Reggio Emilia, a History of the Present*. (English Edition Editor: Peter Moss). Italy: Reggio Children.

The story of the creation and development of the preschools and infant-toddler centres from the perspective of the key protagonists.

Thornton, L. and Brunton, P. (2014) *Understanding the Reggio Approach*, 3rd edition. London: David Fulton Publishers.

An overview of the Reggio Approach which analyses the essential elements of the Reggio Approach and provides examples from the infant-toddler centres and preschools. This is an ideal text for practitioners wishing to extend their understanding of how young children's learning is supported and developed in Reggio Emilia.

Edwards, C. P., Gandini, L. and Forman, G. (eds) (2012) *The Hundred Languages of Children: The Reggio Emilia Experience in Transformation*, 3rd edition. Westport, CT: Albex Publishing.

A collection of interviews with pedagogistas, atelieristas, teachers and administrators from Reggio Emilia, who describe their roles in their own words. This book also contains the transcript of an extended interview with Loris Malaguzzi in which he talks eloquently about the work of the preschools and infant-toddler centres, explaining why things are as they are. Essays and research papers from educators in North America describe how they have been touched by the 'Reggio experience'.

Everyday Utopias (DVD) (2011) Italian dialogue with English subtitles.

A video capturing children's and adults' experiences during a day in the life at an infant-toddler centre and a preschool.

2 | **Relationships**

In the Reggio Approach

A powerful image of the child

Right at the heart of the Reggio Approach is the very powerful image adults have of children. Every child is seen as strong, confident and competent. Strong children have their own ideas, express opinions, make independent choices and are able to play and work well with others.

This powerful image of the child needs adults who listen to children and trust them to make responsible decisions. In the Reggio Approach listening to children involves paying careful attention to what they have to say and think, and taking their ideas seriously.

In Reggio the adults are willing to learn alongside the children. They work together in partnership rather than the adult being 'in charge' and having all the answers. The role of the adult is to plan starting points for the children to explore and to provide open-ended resources which encourage the children to develop their own thinking and ways of learning. The adults watch and listen carefully to what the children do and say and use their observations to guide and extend each child's learning.

Children are encouraged to learn from one another. They work and play together in small groups from a very early age. They learn to listen to each other's points of view and to respect the views and feelings of others.

In Reggio, *all* children are equally important and children with disabilities are welcomed into the infant-toddler centres and preschools. Children with disabilities are referred to as having 'special rights' rather than 'special needs'. This recognises them as strong children who can play a full part in the life of their group.

Two-way relationships

Strong, positive relationships between people lie at the heart of the Reggio Approach. The relationships between teachers and children, parents and teachers, children and parents are two-way relationships. Teachers, children and parents respect each other and listen to each other's point of view.

The diagram below shows the way in which the relationships between children, parents and teachers are seen in Reggio.

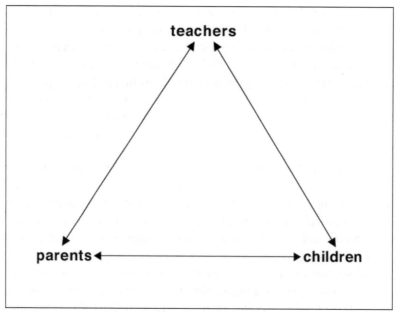

The triangle of relationships

Parents, children and teachers are at each corner of the triangle. They each have their own role to play, and they are all equally important. The arrows show the two-way interactions between the different groups.

Involving parents

Parents have played a central role in the infant-toddler centres and preschools of Reggio Emilia from the very beginning. The first preschools, founded after the Second World War, were a symbol of hope for the future. Since then, parental participation has been at the heart of the development of the Reggio Approach.

The staff at the centres value the important role that parents play in their children's development and learning. Parents are expected to be actively involved in the life of each centre and in return their opinions are respected by staff. Parents take part in group meetings with the teachers, atelieristas and pedagogistas and they also play a role in the management of the centres through their involvement in early childhood councils.

Relationships with the community

Over the last 60 years the relationship between the early childhood centres and the city of Reggio Emilia has grown and developed. The municipality invests money in the preschools and infant-toddler centres and in services for families. In turn, the early childhood centres see it as their responsibility to nurture good citizens of today, and of the future. The centres take every opportunity to tell the local community about their work, often by displaying the children's projects, thoughts and artwork in shops, theatres, parks and in the streets of the city.

In the Reggio Approach children learn how to behave as responsible members of society. Here, society means the child's family, the adults and children in their infant-toddler centre or preschool as well as the wider community in which they live. The powerful children of Reggio Emilia are helped to understand that they have duties and responsibilities as well as rights. The routines within the early childhood centres are designed not only to respect children's rights, but also to give them opportunities to be responsible and carry out their duties.

Quality practice in the Early Years Foundation Stage

Relationships are an important value of the Reggio Approach. Our own curriculum guidance documents in the UK put an emphasis on the quality of relationships between children and adults, recognising that children learn to be strong and independent through positive relationships. Parents are recognised as children's first educators and parents and practitioners working together well helps children to develop as well-rounded individuals.

In the EYFS framework, personal, social and emotional development (PSED) is highlighted as one of the three prime areas of learning and development. It involves helping children to develop a positive sense of themselves, and others; to form positive relationships and develop respect for others; to develop social skills and learn how to manage their feelings; to understand appropriate behaviour in groups; and to have confidence in their own abilities.

Respecting each other

Every interaction is based on caring professional relationships and respectful acknowledgement of the feelings of children and their families. This involves:

- Respect for others as the basis of good relationships.

- Understanding that babies and children learn who they are and what they can accomplish through relationships.

- Helping children to learn about others through their relationships, becoming aware that others may have different needs, feelings and ideas from their own.

- Encouraging friendships so that children learn interpersonal skills and start to appreciate that there are other viewpoints besides their own.

- Supporting effective relationships which foster children's emotional and social development.

- Recognising that responsive, supportive, warm and respectful relationships between children are bolstered when these qualities feature in interactions between adults.

- Developing good relationships between practitioners and parents to build on family and cultural practices when tuning in to children's needs and ideas.

Parents as partners

Parents are children's first and most enduring educators. When parents and practitioners work together in early years settings, the results have a positive impact on children's development and learning.

To develop effective partnerships with parents it is important for practitioners to recognise that:

- Parents provide a learning environment which is enduring and comprehensive.

- Home and community are significant learning environments in the lives of children.

- All parents can enhance their child's development and learning.

- Parents have the right to play a central role in making decisions about their child's care and education at every level.

- Successful relationships between parents and educators can have long-lasting and beneficial effects on children's learning and well-being.

Supporting learning

Warm, trusting relationships with knowledgeable adults support children's learning more effectively than any amount of resources.

The key messages to think about here are:

- Bringing together knowledge about individual children and knowledge about what they can learn enables practitioners to plan and provide for meaningful next steps in learning.

- Adult support in the EYFS should include scope for independent learning, timely guidance and ongoing reassurance and encouragement to enable young children to feel secure, valued and individually well cared for. There should be a balance of child-initiated and adult-initiated activities.

- Children learn best through their interactions with people who know and relate to them well.

- Practitioners should place great store on listening to what parents say about their children's needs and how they make themselves understood.

- Listening to children enables practitioners to create meaningful activities that help them to make connections and tackle new ideas.

- Children develop their own thinking and encounter new ideas when they have the opportunity to engage in play in which they take the lead and make choices.

Key person

Each child must have a key person who has special responsibilities for working with a small number of children, giving them the reassurance to feel safe and cared for. The key person's role is to help ensure that every child's care is tailored to meet their individual needs, to help the child become familiar with the setting, offer a settled relationship for the child and build a relationship with their parents. The key person has a responsibility to engage and support parents and/or carers in guiding their child's development at home and should also help families engage with more specialist support if appropriate.

The important principles behind the key person approach are:

- The key person makes sure that each child for whom they have special responsibility feels individual, cherished and thought about by someone, in particular while they are away from home.

- The key person can help parents to build a partnership with professional staff and make sure that parents know about their child's day.

- The key person is likely to have a powerful impact on a child's well-being, their mental health and their opportunities to think and learn.

Inspiration from the Reggio Approach

In the infant-toddler centres and preschools of Reggio Emilia two-way relationships are of great importance. To the visitor it is clear that teamwork plays an essential part in the daily life of the centres. Practitioners from the UK who have visited Reggio, and been inspired by what they saw, have looked at different ways to improve the quality of relationships in their setting.

The areas they have thought about are:

- having a shared image of the child;

- working together and valuing relationships;

- active listening;

- consulting with children;

- involving parents;

- relationships with the community.

Having a shared image of the child

For a staff team to work together successfully you must agree an image of the child that you can all share. You will need to set aside time to do this together. All of us have an image of how we think children should be. We will have formed this image in many different ways – the way we were brought up ourselves, what we have learned about young children and what we have seen happening in practice. Remember it is important that all staff have an opportunity to share their views of children and childhood.

The EYFS Framework (2012) recognises that every child is a unique child, who is constantly learning and can be resilient, capable, confident and self-assured. This requires practitioners to view children as competent, confident individuals, respecting children and listening to their ideas and opinions. It involves encouraging them to be independent, to make choices and try things out.

As a team you will need to decide how to do this in practice. You will need to think about:

- how all staff engage with children;

- the language, including body language, you use;

- the role models you provide;

- how you provide opportunities for independence;

- giving 'real' choices to children and supporting the choices they make;

- allowing risky freedom.

Competent, confident children ask lots of questions and can be challenging to be with. It is important that you share your image of the child with parents so that the children receive consistent messages at home and in your setting.

Your image of the strong child has to be very easily seen in all your daily routines and practices. You will probably need to review your setting's policies to make sure they reflect this.

When you are appointing new staff use the interview to share the image you have of children and to make sure they can sign up to it.

Working together and valuing relationships

Teamwork and cooperation make an enormous contribution to enjoyable and effective learning for children and adults. Providing opportunities for children and adults to work together as part of a group, each making their own contribution, helps children to recognise and value the knowledge which different individuals have. Children of different ages can work together, learning from one another and sharing skills.

Children learn how to build relationships by copying the behaviour of the adults around them. By cooperating well with colleagues, speaking politely to them and being interested in what they have to say, you can provide a good role model for children to follow. Adults working as part of a team can share observations and use their combined experience to plan together how best to extend children's learning.

Active listening

Active listening involves showing that you are interested in what children have to say. Some children will be able to express their ideas and feelings easily in words, but others may find this more difficult. They may be too young to use language or they may not yet have mastered the technicalities of putting complex thoughts and ideas together in words. Other children may not have the confidence to speak out.

For all children it is important to pay careful attention to the many different ways they use to communicate. This could be by their facial expression, their body language, how they stand or move, or how they behave in a particular situation.

Making time to listen to children can be planned in as a part of your daily organisation and routines. At the beginning of the morning or afternoon the children could come together as a group to discuss what they are going to do during the session. This gives children an opportunity to talk about things that are important to them and to think about how to organise their ideas. This is an opportunity for you to model how to listen carefully to help children to learn to listen to one another.

Asking questions without using words

Where this group meeting happens is important. It needs to be some-where where everyone can sit comfortably, can hear one another, and where you won't be interrupted.

Talking and listening together in a group also helps children to learn how to negotiate with one another and agree how to share equipment and resources. Shared plans, negotiated and agreed at the beginning of the session can always be referred back to later in the day if any conflict arises. These then become practical opportunities to reinforce teamwork and cooperation and show children the importance of individual rights, duties and responsibilities.

Active listening can take place anywhere – indoors or outdoors. Remember there are many opportunities for extending children's play and learning when they are outdoors. You can do this by listening to and watching what is going on around you and then intervening appropriately.

Consulting with children

Children have views and opinions about the setting they are in, the organisation of their day and the resources and equipment that they have to use. They may express these opinions in various ways – through avoiding areas of the setting, ignoring certain resources or showing that they enjoy some aspects of their daily routine more than others. Consulting with children and encouraging them to tell you about their likes and dislikes is a very obvious way of showing that you value what they have to tell you.

You could ask for their ideas and opinions by talking with them, or you could help them to use a camera to take photographs of places they like and places they don't like. Talking together about these photographs will help you think together about why the layout and routines of the setting are arranged in a particular way. This will help children to appreciate why some things are as they are as well as to identify things which could be changed.

Remember, if you consult with children, and ask them for their ideas about things, you have to be prepared to change things in response to what they tell you.

Involving parents

Developing strong positive relationships between parents and early years staff is an essential part of supporting young children's learning and development. Parents have unique knowledge about their child which you will want them to share with you. When a child first joins your setting spend time talking to the parents and listen carefully to the words they use to describe their child. Listening to parents will give you an insight into how they view their child – for example, 'Is he/she confident, outgoing, talkative, friendly, shy, quiet, thoughtful, or self-conscious?' This information will help you to provide the correct environment and support to enable the child to settle well and enjoy the experiences available to them. Take full account of cultural differences and work hard to ensure that all children see positive images around the setting with which they can directly identify.

In return, parents are entitled to as much information as possible about your approach to working with children. Be aware that some parents will be more comfortable than others with understanding your approach and may need lots of encouragement and support. Provide parents with clear, straightforward information about what happens in your setting, how the space is laid out and how the day is organised. An 'identity card' with pictures of the staff, a plan of the building and the routine of a typical day will help parents to feel part of the life of the setting.

Presenting information for parents in an interesting and attractive way

Photographs and children's comments recorded during the course of the day can be put into a 'daily diary' positioned where parents and carers pick children up at the end of the day. Looking at this information before they collect their child will give parents a starting point for a conversation with their child about what they have been doing during the day.

Involving parents in projects carried out in the setting gives them a greater understanding of how young children learn. It also allows you to draw on a wide range of expertise and experience.

Relationships with the community

It is important for children who attend your setting to be aware of the wider community they live in. This is particularly important for those children who attend your setting regularly, from an early age, and spend the whole day with you. In the revised EYFS (2012), building children's awareness of the community in which they live is emphasised in the restructured specific area of learning, 'Understanding the world'.

Taking children out to explore the local environment is one simple way you can make them more aware of the wider world. You could go out regularly to visit a local park or green space. If your setting is in a town you could take a group of children out to explore the built environment all around them – the houses, shops and public buildings around their setting. Planning regular visits to the same place at different times of year will help children to appreciate the changes which happen through the seasons. Outside visits need careful planning and a thorough risk assessment. Spend time talking to parents so they understand why you feel it is important to take children out and how this supports their learning and development.

Children's understanding of the community they live in can be encouraged by inviting visitors in to your setting. These might be people who live and work locally, people who do particular jobs, or representatives of different ethnic groups. Again, you will need to plan carefully to make these visits a success for everyone – the children, the

Helping children to learn about the world of work

visitor and the staff team. Helping children to learn about the world of work, and the different jobs which people do, will all support their growing understanding of what it means to be a citizen in a community.

It is equally important that the local community understands about the work which you do in caring for and supporting the development of young children. There are opportunities to do this through becoming involved in community events, arranging for children's pictures, drawings, models and projects to be displayed in public buildings such as the library, the tourist information centre or the town hall. Think about possibilities for linking up with businesses and firms which the children's parents work for.

In Reggio Emilia they feel so strongly that the work of the infant-toddler centres and preschools should be visible to the people who live in the city that they use the expression, 'The city of the children, the city for the children'.

Snapshot

This snapshot demonstrates how listening to children, respecting their ideas and working cooperatively with colleagues and parents can bring huge rewards for everyone.

Remodelling the garden

In a preschool a discussion between staff about the garden and how it was currently used led to an outline plan to redesign the outdoor space.

In small groups the children went for a walk around the garden and were encouraged to think about the things they would like to be able to do outside. This discussion went on for over a week to give the children time to think about different possibilities and to develop their ideas. At the same time parents were informed about the garden project and invited to input their ideas, skills and experience.

The children came up with many different ideas, some more practical and feasible than others. Adults and children spent time discussing all the different ideas and eventually agreed on a small range of projects, some of which could be started immediately, and others which would take longer to carry out. The children were quick to volunteer the skills of their parents to assist.

One idea, popular with many of the children, focused on making a 'reading den' in a corner of the garden – a wooden base and frame which could be draped with fabric to create a special place to look at books, or play with toys and friends. Parents and staff provided the woodworking skills to build the frame. One member of staff worked with a small group of children to plant up the adjacent border with scented plants and herbs, donated by the local garden centre.

The reading den quickly became a favourite place for children to play outside, changing its identity from a shop to a den to a tent to a garage, to a boat to a space rocket, depending on the interests of the group using it.

The offcuts of wood from the frame had been stacked in a low pile nearby, along with some large stones and a rotten branch. Within two weeks the area was a rich source of insects, spiders, worms and woodlice.

Children and staff then worked together to devise 'ground rules' for the use of the 'reading den'. These helped to ensure that everyone had a chance to use the den and that the plants and the log pile were respected and not disturbed.

Throughout the project staff took photographs and noted the children's comments and ideas. This information was put together in a documentation panel which was displayed in the local library.

Reference

DfE (2012) *Statutory Framework for the Early Years Foundation Stage: Setting the standards for learning, development and care for children from birth to five.*

Further reading

Strozzi, P. and Vecchi, V. (eds) (2002) *Advisories.* Italy: Reggio Children.

Five- and 6-year-old children from the Diana school tell incoming 3-year-olds about their new preschool. This publication gives a wonderful insight into the Reggio experience as seen through the eyes of the children.

Davoli, M. and Ferri, G. (eds) (2000) *Reggio Tutta: A Guide to the City by the Children.* Italy: Reggio Children.

A description of a long-term project involving all the preschools and infant-toddler centres in Reggio Emilia. An example of the strong relationships which exist between the children of Reggio Emilia and the city itself.

Questions to think about

A shared image of the child

- Have we spent time coming to a shared understanding of our image of the child?

- Do we understand what this means in practice?

- Do we provide opportunities for children to make decisions and be responsible?

- Are we good role models for children, colleagues and parents?

Relationships with parents

- How do we show parents that we value them and the role they play?

- Do we use photographs and written comments to help parents understand young children's learning?

- Do we listen well to what parents have to say to us?

- Have we spent time planning and developing our 'key person' approach?

Relationships with the community

- How well do we understand our place in the community?

- How do we help children to become aware of this?

- What opportunities could we use to improve the local community's understanding of what we do?

- Do we use visits, visitors, outings and events to help children see their place in the community?

3 | Creativity

In the Reggio Approach

Creativity and the languages of expression

Loris Malaguzzi's ideas about creativity and creative children have shaped the development of the Reggio Approach. Malaguzzi believed that all children are naturally creative and that they should have opportunities to develop their creative skills and expression. It was also his idea to have an atelier, a studio, in each centre and to include an atelierista, a person with particular creative skills, as a member of staff.

When Loris Malaguzzi talked about children's learning he used the expression 'the hundred languages of children'. This recognises that creative children have many different ways of expressing themselves. Malaguzzi emphasised that adults should listen carefully to the many different languages that children use – including talking, singing, dancing, painting, drawing and performing.

In Reggio, creativity is at the heart of all learning experiences for young children. It is not tied to any particular area of the curriculum, but instead is a way of thinking, knowing and making choices and can be demonstrated in any aspect of learning.

The Reggio Approach encourages the development of children's creativity by providing:

- open-ended resources;

- a rich variety of experiences;
- space to explore materials;
- time to develop ideas;
- freedom to solve problems and try things out;
- the opportunity to learn skills;
- adults as role models of creativity.

Intelligent materials

To support young children's creative expression teachers in Reggio pay careful attention to the types of resources they provide for the children. In both the infant-toddler centres and the preschools there are very few 'toys' which have only one purpose. Instead the centres are stocked with a wide range of open-ended resources which children can explore and use creatively.

Many of these are natural resources and include wood, stone, shells, cones, seeds and leaves. Alongside these are materials which come from the creative recycling centre in Reggio Emilia known as Remida. Children have access to beads, glass, bottles, paper, card, tubing, fabric, plastic and metal.

The term 'intelligent materials' is used to refer to this vast range of creative resources. This encourages children to think of them as valuable and full of potential, ready to be transformed into any manner of new creations and inventions.

From a very young age babies and children in the infant-toddler centres and preschools are helped to develop their skills in working with clay and wire. These two materials not only help to develop children's manipulative skills, they also encourage children to use their imagination.

The exhibition of the work of the preschools of Reggio Emilia, which tours the world, is called The Wonder of Learning – The Hundred Languages of Children. It is a wonderful example of what creative young children can think, say and do.

Quality practice in the Early Years Foundation Stage

Nurturing and celebrating children's creative expression of ideas, thoughts and feelings is fundamental to the way in which educators in Reggio support and develop young children's learning. Being creative means using knowledge and skills to make connections between different areas of learning, and putting ideas together in new and unusual ways. Creativity – creating and thinking critically – is important across all areas of learning and development and, along with playing and exploring and active learning, is one of the three characteristics of effective learning in the revised EYFS Framework (2012).

In addition, expressive arts and design (EAD) is one of the specific areas of learning and development. This involves enabling children to explore and play with a wide range of media and materials, as well as providing opportunities and encouragement for sharing their thoughts, ideas and feelings through a variety of activities in art, music, movement, dance, role play, and design and technology.

Creating and thinking critically

This characteristic of effective learning recognises that children of all ages, from babyhood onwards, have their own ideas, use what they already know to learn new things and choose new and unique ways of doing things.

- *Children having their own ideas* is about coming up with new ideas or ways of doing things across all areas of learning and development. By being inventive and creative, children find new challenges and problems to solve and come up with their own unique ways of solving these.

- *Using what they already know to learn new things* begins when very young babies begin to notice patterns based on the sensory input they gain from their environment, and then start to make predictions based on this information. As children grow older, their thinking becomes more conscious as they develop concepts and begin to link them together. As their thinking develops children begin to find meaning in sequence, in cause and effect, and in the intentions of others.

- *Choosing ways to do things and finding new ways* is all about how children learn to approach goal-directed activity in organised ways by making choices and decisions about how to approach tasks. This involves planning what to do and being able to change their approach if necessary.

Inspiration from the Reggio Approach

Creating a climate for creativity

In the Reggio Approach creativity is about having ideas, using imagination and solving problems. Creativity is not just linked to art, music and dance; it is a part of all areas of learning. Children can be creative when they explore language, mathematics, construction, scientific exploration and design technology.

To support young children's creativity it is important to think about how you can:

- listen to children's different languages of expression;

- value 'creative spaces', indoors and outdoors;

- provide open-ended resources;

- encourage, and manage, opportunities for risk and challenge.

Languages of expression

Children communicate their thinking not just through what they say, but also through painting, drawing, construction, role play, small-world play, movement, music making, singing, dancing, exploring and problem solving. These are all the activities that take place daily in a high-quality early years setting.

Being aware of all these different languages of expression means we need to see the value of all the different aspects which make up children's play. This will involve ideas developed by the children from their own experiences as well as activities planned by you as a practitioner, and could be happening indoors or outdoors.

As adults we all have different interests and talents and will naturally find it easier to connect more easily with some aspects of children's play than others. For example:

- the outdoor enthusiast will see the value of digging in the garden and finding earthworms;

- the musically talented will appreciate a baby's attempts to use different resources as a drum;

- the practically minded will value the importance of children exploring how different materials behave when you try to build with them.

In addition, we all approach learning in different ways. Some of us will be largely visual learners and rely heavily on using our eyes, and on illustrations and pictures to make sense of the world. Others will be auditory learners and will prefer to use our ears to hear information and instructions. Others will be largely kinaesthetic learners and will learn best when able to feel and handle objects and to move around to physically experience things with our bodies.

To support young children's learning it is important to understand the value of all these different types of experiences and learning preferences in young children's development.

This involves:

- making sure the daily activities and opportunities planned for the children provide a wide variety of experiences;

- guarding against accidentally giving out messages to children, or parents, that some activities, experiences or forms of expression are more important than others;

- paying attention to the different ways in which individual children approach their learning, not assuming that everyone learns in the same way as we do.

Creative spaces

In some settings it may be possible to have a separate room as a studio, but in all settings, children's creativity can be encouraged and supported by taking care over the way you arrange your environment, indoors and out. In Chapter 4 you can find some ideas about how to make use of light, shadow, colour and reflection in the design of different areas of your setting.

A creative area in your setting should be a place where children can:

- use high-quality art materials for drawing, painting and modelling;

- learn the skills of using resources and materials creatively;

- store part-finished projects and display 'work in progress';

- learn the value of storing and displaying open-ended resources and materials in an orderly and beautiful way.

Using high-quality art materials

Providing children with a range of different art materials to represent their ideas and theories (Chapter 6) will help them to explore their thinking in different ways. In some situations it will be more appro-priate to provide fine paintbrushes, pens and pencils rather than 'fat' brushes and chunky crayons. 'Fat paintbrushes' produce 'fat paintings', when sometimes a child may want to record the fine detail in the picture they are creating. Think about the range of paint colour choices you offer to children. Sometimes it may be better to offer:

- fewer choices of colour;

- less vibrant colours and more pastel shades;

- several shades of the same colour – think about how you could help children to investigate subtle colour mixing.

Covering easels and tables with newspaper to protect them is common practice – newspaper is cheap and easily disposed of. However it can also be messy, provides a very dull background and can distract from the work a child is involved in. Using plain lining paper instead gives a powerful message to children about how much you value their creative efforts.

Learning creative skills

With all creative resources and equipment for children – drawing and painting materials, clay and dough, cutting and joining tools and musical instruments – it is important for children to be taught the skills they need to use the materials creatively and safely.

Children will only understand the many different ways in which clay can be manipulated – by pushing, prodding, squeezing, squashing, rolling, cutting and joining – when they have had the opportunity to watch an adult, or another child, working clay in all these different ways.

Using interesting tools to manipulate and shape clay

Displaying work in progress

Learning from the Reggio Approach will involve you in helping children to develop some of their ideas and explorations over an extended period of time. They will need to be able to store things safely so they can come back to them at a later date.

Organising your creative area so that you can display children's work in progress will demonstrate to everyone – children, staff and parents – how much you value their ideas. These displays can become an important and constantly changing part of the environment of your setting. Displaying these part-finished projects will encourage other children and adults to comment, ask questions and become involved.

Storing and displaying resources

When you are collecting together reclaimed resources and equipping your creative space think about how you will store and display them. For children to use them creatively they need to be attractively presented and easily accessible. If children cannot see things or find them easily they won't be able to use them.

Referring to reclaimed materials as 'junk' or 'scrap' and paying little attention to how they are stored and presented to the children is unlikely to encourage them to value and respect these resources.

Think about the contrasts in the following situations:

- a shelf containing sets of empty boxes, some circular, some rectangular, stacked neatly on top of one another in size order;

- the same boxes pushed one on top of another into a plastic dustbin.

Which do you think is likely to stimulate children's creativity more?

Displaying natural and reclaimed materials attractively
encourages children to use them creatively

Creativity outdoors

A creative space can be set up outdoors as well as indoors. It provides an opportunity for children to use skills and experiences in a different context and so make links in their learning. Outdoors children can explore, investigate, construct and be creative on a larger scale than they can indoors.

There are many different ways you could set up your outdoor creative space. You may decide to:

- set it up with magnifiers, art materials, chalks, paints, charcoal and easels and encourage children to look closely at the natural world;

- provide a wide range of natural and recycled materials – wood, gravel, sand, leaves, grasses, seeds, cones, fabric strips, plastic bottles, twine and hessian for pattern making, mosaics and weaving;

- stock the space with large pieces of wood, planks, crates, guttering, pipes, fabric sheets, ropes, boxes, buckets and tubes for building large-scale constructions and dens;

- use it as a space where children can investigate shadows, 'painting with water' or reflections in a puddle;

- use it as an outdoor performance area – for stories, role play, music making and dance.

Open-ended resources

Offering a wide range of open-ended resources to children to investigate and use will encourage them to use their imagination and creativity. From a very young age they will build up their understanding of different materials by exploring what they look like, what they smell like, what they taste like, what they feel like and how they behave when you poke or prod them, or wave them around.

An outdoor performance area built from locally resourced materials

Babies and toddlers

A collection of baskets containing everyday objects and carefully selected natural materials will give babies and toddlers many different creative opportunities. You can vary the contents of the baskets to suit the age of the children and change the collection depending on the particular experiences you are focusing on.

Everyday objects you could use for babies include:

- kitchen tools: wooden, plastic and metal spoons of different sizes, rolling pin, sieve, pastry brush, jelly mould, salad servers;

- bathroom accessories: nailbrush, small flannel, sponge, loofah, plastic duck, pumice stone, hairbrush, toothbrush, bath plug and chain;

- fabrics: towelling, knitted material, fleece, a piece of cotton, carpet tile, chiffon, net curtain material, silk fabric.

Collections for toddlers can include:

- materials: large pebbles, driftwood, small offcuts of wood, cork mat, glass paperweight, plastic cup, rubber ball, metal bowl, small china dish, paper plate;
- scented collection: sprigs of lavender, lemon or orange, soaps, scented candle, herbs, empty perfume bottles;
- natural materials: shells, large pebbles or polished stones, pine cones of different sizes, leaves of different shapes, twigs, sand, large seed pods, conkers, pieces of tree bark.

As with all the other resources in your setting you would need to check these collections of resources regularly to make sure they are safe and clean, and to supervise children when they are using them.

Three- to 5-year-old children

For older children open-ended resources provide interesting starting points for all sorts of creative ideas. Natural materials such as wood, stone, leaves, cones, seedpods, bark, cork, shells and sand can be used for construction, for sorting and classifying, for measuring and counting and for pattern making. A collection of conkers, shells or polished stones is just as useful a counting set as a tub of plastic counters or mini dinosaurs.

Recycled materials are often available at very little cost from your local creative recycling centre. These resources provide you with a wealth of interesting materials for children to use. The sorts of resources you can obtain include offcuts of wood, plastic tubing, paper and card of different thicknesses and textures, plastic discs, metal washers and springs, zips, buttons, fabric samples, wool and thread, plastic cones, cardboard and leather offcuts.

Resources can be attractively presented outdoors as well as indoors

Think carefully how you present these resources to the children. The more attractively they are presented, the more likely the children are to use the resources creatively. Perhaps you could set them out in clear plastic trays arranged in colour-coded patterns, similar to the arrangement you find in a paint or fabric colour chart. This attention to detail will show the children how much you value the materials, will encourage them to choose and use them creatively and to clear them away carefully when they have finished.

Managing risky freedom

To be creative children have to feel confident to take risks and try things out. Part of this will involve them 'taking risks' with their ideas. This means being confident to ask questions and put forward ideas without being afraid that people will either laugh at them or tell them they are wrong. You can develop this 'climate for creativity' through the way you build children's self-confidence and self-respect by being an active listener and a good role model.

Encouraging children to 'try things out' involves you being comfortable with what is known as 'risky freedom'. To learn fully about the world they live in it is very important for them to have the opportunity for all sorts of different 'guided experiences'. These 'guided experiences' might include finding out how to handle a glass object safely, learning how to climb a ladder or a set of steps, being shown how to saw a piece of wood or hammer in a nail safely. These experiences all carry an element of risk but being aware of what risk is, and how to manage it, is an essential part of children developing an appreciation of danger.

Risk in any situation can be minimised by carrying out a thorough risk assessment. Remember risk assessments are there to make experiences and activities as safe as possible; they are not intended to be used as an excuse for not doing things.

Snapshot

The following snapshot demonstrates what creative expression might look like with very young children.

Toddlers, tubes and boxes

A toddler is sitting on the carpet surrounded by a set of small boxes which nest inside one another, a pine cone, a cardboard poster tube and a large chiffon scarf. Her key person is sitting opposite her, watching, talking to the toddler about what she is doing, but not intervening.

The toddler investigates the boxes one by one, trying to put the pine cone into each one in turn. After a long time trying things out she puts the pine cone in the middle-sized box and puts the lid on. She puts the lid on the largest box and offers it to her key person.

A delightful creative game with a scarf and a tube

Discovering the box is empty the adult pretends to be disappointed. The toddler takes the box back, wraps the middle-size box up in the chiffon scarf and offers this to the practitioner as a present. The game continues for some time, exchanging boxes back and forth.

Next, the cardboard tube is added to the toddler's play. The key person drops the pine cone into the open end of the tube and expresses great surprise when it rolls out of the other end. The toddler abandons the boxes and scarf and plays for some time with the cone and tube – discovering along the way what happens when you hit yourself on the head with a cardboard tube.

The practitioner mimes peering down the tube and the toddler copies this. She then in turn mimes speaking into the tube and putting it to her ear. This game with the tube continues for some time until the adult pushes the chiffon scarf into the open end of the tube. The toddler pulls the scarf out, drops it over her head and collapses in a fit of giggles.

The whole interaction has lasted about half an hour; several times during the encounter the nursery manager used a digital camera to record what was happening. These pictures will be shared with the child's parents at the end of the day. A written comment from the key person describing the context of the encounter will be added to the pictures before including them in the display on the wall of the nursery. Later in the week the encounter will be used in a staff meeting to develop the team's understanding of young children's learning.

Reference

DfE (2012) *Statutory Framework for the Early Years Foundation Stage: Setting the standards for learning, development and care for children from birth to five.*

Further reading

Vecchi, V. and Giudici, C. (eds) (2004) *Children, Art, Artists: The Expressive Languages of Children: The artistic language of Alberto Burri.* Italy: Reggio Children.

This book tells the story of a series of projects involving children from infant-toddler (0–3 years) to middle school age (8–9 years). It contains detailed descriptions and illustrations of young children's interactions with natural and recycled materials. The second part of the book contains a series of essays which look at the role of children's creativity in the Reggio Approach.

Questions to think about

Valuing children's creativity

- Do we understand what creativity means?

- How do we recognise and value our own creativity?

- Do we give children enough time and opportunity to develop their creative expression across all areas of learning?

- How do we demonstrate that we value the different languages of expression that children use?

Developing creative places

- Do we pay enough attention to the way the environment is set out to encourage children's creativity?

- Do we provide children with a wide range of high-quality 'art materials' so they can represent their ideas?

- Is children's 'work in progress' well presented and displayed?

- Have we developed our outdoor spaces so they encourage creative expression?

Providing open-ended resources

- Do we give children resources which will stimulate their creativity?

- Are the resources presented attractively?

- Do we make enough use of freely available natural resources?

- How do we encourage, and manage, opportunities for risk and challenge?

4 | The environment

In the Reggio Approach

The environment as the third teacher

The quality of the environment in the infant-toddler centres and preschools is an important value of the Reggio Approach. It plays an active role in how children play and learn. The environment includes the building itself, how the rooms are organised, what they look like and what resources and equipment they have in them. The two teachers working with each class or group think that the environment is so important that they call it 'the third teacher'. This expression recognises that the environment is such a high priority that organising it well is the equivalent of having a third teacher in the room.

By planning the environment carefully teachers show clearly what they value for young children and their families. The entrance areas are welcoming, the layout is tidy and practical and the atmosphere is calm and joyful. Open-ended resources and equipment encourage curiosity, creativity and communication. Photographs and descriptions on the walls tell the stories of children's learning journeys. The overall impression is of a beautiful place to be.

Every space has a purpose

Some of the early childhood centres are purpose-built and others are found in refurbished buildings. They all include small spaces, large open spaces, thresholds between the inside and outside, and outdoor areas. In Reggio educators pay close attention to the use of space and use the expression 'every space has a purpose'. This involves looking carefully at how different spaces are planned and used.

For **children** there are spaces where they can:

- be creative;
- make choices;
- explore and investigate;
- think and reflect;
- be involved in projects;
- communicate;
- have privacy.

For **teachers** there are spaces where they can:

- meet with colleagues to share observations and plans;
- study;
- have privacy.

For **parents** there are spaces where they can:

- share their children's learning;
- meet with others;
- make their views known;
- join in the life of the centre.

A typical 'Reggio school'

As well as the home bases for groups of children, which in Reggio are called classrooms or sections, each building also has a number of special rooms.

These special rooms are the piazza, the atelier, the kitchen and dining room and the courtyard. They are modelled on the squares, galleries, restaurants and parks of the city of Reggio Emilia.

The **piazza** is a large space in the middle of the building where children of different ages meet and play together. Large equipment such as kaleidoscope mirrors, dressing-up capsules and puppet theatres are found in the piazza.

The **atelier**, or studio, is usually found off the piazza. This is where groups of children take part in creative activity with the atelierista on a daily basis. The atelier is equipped with a wide range of creative resources, including clay, art materials, reclaimed and natural materials. A mini atelier is also attached to each classroom.

The **kitchen** and the **dining areas** are very important parts of the centres. Mealtimes are seen as valuable opportunities for the children's personal and social development. Tables are laid out by the children with tablecloths, flowers and real crockery, glasses and cutlery. The kitchen staff play a vital role in the life of the centres and large windows between the kitchen and the rest of the centre allow the children to see them preparing meals.

The **courtyard** is an open-air space next to the piazza which the children can access at all times. It creates an indoor/outdoor space. In Reggio the courtyard is called the 'classroom without a roof'.

Quality practice in the Early Years Foundation Stage

In Reggio the architecture of the buildings and the layout of the rooms all support the philosophy behind the Reggio Approach. The spaces are designed to allow each child, and each group of children, to have daily opportunities to play, to explore and discover, to communicate and to develop relationships.

The enabling environment is one of the four guiding principles of the revised EYFS framework which should guide quality practice in an early years setting. Children learn and develop well in enabling environments in which their experiences respond to their individual needs and there is a strong partnership between practitioners and parents and/or carers.

The learning environment

A rich and varied environment supports children's learning and development. It gives them confidence to explore and learn in secure and safe, yet challenging, indoor and outdoor spaces.

The key principles behind organising the environment are:

- Babies, toddlers and young children thrive in an environment that supports and promotes their active learning and development.

- Young children require space, indoors and outdoors, where they can be active or quiet, and where they can think, dream and watch others.

- The space needs to be appropriate for the age and development of all the children so that they can have suitable access to it and can interact within it.

- In deciding what is an 'appropriate environment' it is important to understand the way babies, toddlers and young children learn and to provide for the age and stage of the children concerned.

- There is no 'ideal' environment as babies' and young children's interests change, and the environment should change in response to these changing interests.

- The space needs to be secure, appropriately heated and aired and free from hazards.

- There need to be well-organised areas and resources, both natural and manufactured, which are accessible to the children.

- There should be opportunities for a range of activities such as soft play, paint mixing, growing plants, mark making, looking at books, reading stories, or exploring the properties of materials such as clay, sand or water.

- The space, both indoors and outdoors, should preferably be available all the time so children can choose activities and follow their interests.

- Outdoor learning is enhanced by an environment that is richly resourced with play materials that can be adapted and used in different ways.

- Children need the support of attentive and engaged adults who are enthusiastic about the outdoors and understand the importance of outdoor learning.

- The outdoor space needs to offer shade and shelter, and children should have opportunities to experience changing seasons and the passing of time.

Inspiration from the Reggio Approach

In all the infant-toddler centres and preschools in Reggio Emilia the same design features can be seen. The beautiful and striking environments make a lasting impression on everyone who visits Reggio. Many practitioners from the UK have been inspired to re-examine the layout and design of their own environments to see how they can be changed to fully support the requirements of the EYFS framework. The features they have looked at are:

- visibility;
- flexibility;
- light and shadow;
- reflection;
- multi-sensory spaces.

Visibility

Being able to see in and out of rooms helps us to see ourselves as part of a wider community. We can see what is happening elsewhere and feel connected to everyone and everything in our setting. It stops us feeling cut off from children and staff in other rooms and from the outside world.

When centres are being designed or refurbished it is possible to look at different ways of dividing off rooms and spaces. Walls can be half-height, made partly of transparent materials or have internal windows. Porthole windows in doors, at child and adult height, can give glimpses of what is happening beyond the home base. Doors can be replaced by open archways or 'saloon' doors.

As adults, we appreciate how being able to see out of windows is important for emotional well-being. We feel comfortable knowing what is happening outside, being aware of the time of day, the weather and the seasons. Most buildings we live and work in have windows positioned so that adults can do this. We need to consider ways of making sure that children too are able to observe the world outside. If your setting has high windows think about replacing them with lower windows or patio doors. If that isn't possible try raising the floor level by building a fixed platform area for children to stand on.

There are very simple things we can do to ensure that we make the most of the visibility we have. Draw children's attention to things that are visible outside. Make sure that you lift babies and toddlers up to see out of the windows. Avoid covering the windows with pictures and paintings; use voile if you need to screen large windows from public view.

Flexibility

Different groups of children and staff will have their own ideas about the environment they like to play and work in. Some areas of the room may be fixed, for example the area where water is explored, but most spaces can be changed and used for different purposes at different times.

Instead of using fixed items of furniture to create areas within the room try open shelving, clear perspex screens or large weaving frames as room dividers. Areas for rest and sleep can be softened and the ceiling lowered by using lightweight drapes and canopies.

Rooms filled with fixed furniture, tables and chairs leave little opportunity for flexibility or space for children to move around. Think carefully about how many tables and chairs you need to have in a room and look at other possibilities for some activities – would children be more comfortable playing on the floor, or at a low table or platform?

Is there an area in the room where children can build a den? Den building – using frames, sheets or blankets – is an important way for children to have an element of control over the environment they are in. They can choose and use the den building materials independently and learn to cooperate together as a team during the building process. The den itself then becomes an ideal place for children to play together in small groups, encouraging communication and fostering relationships.

Many settings have looked at ways to provide more flexibility by increasing children's use of the outdoors. This includes opening doors and giving children free access to the outdoor area as well as placing resources and activities that are traditionally used indoors in the outdoor area. This can include mark making and creative materials, small-world play toys and props for imaginative play.

Children who attend the setting regularly throughout the year may spend a lot of time in a room base; it becomes a home away from home for them. Talking to them about how the room is laid out, and what they like (and dislike) about it will help them feel an important part of the setting. Changing the appearance of the room on a regular basis helps to keep it fresh and exciting – for adults and children alike.

Light and shadow

As adults we are all conscious of light and shadow, but perhaps take them too much for granted. Light and shadow are resources which young children find fascinating, and they are available for next to nothing.

Large, low placed windows give children lots of opportunities to experience natural light and to become aware of shadows. Look around your setting at different times of day and see where the sun comes into the room. Then draw children's attention to the sunlight as it moves slowly across the room. Puzzling out why this happens is a wonderful way of encouraging children to come up with ideas and to try to explain them. Help the children to notice the shadows that different objects make when the sun shines on them. Discuss their size, their shape, their colour, and why they change.

Investigating shadows outdoors provides endless variety and encourages children to look more closely at their surroundings. Different areas of the outdoor space will be in shadow at different times of day, and shadows themselves vary through the day. Sometimes they are small and fat, other times long and thin. They may be ahead, behind, or alongside, but they are always there whenever the sun is shining.

Using dimmer switches means that light levels in some areas of the room can be brought right down. This gives children the chance to experience the magic of darkness and provides the contrast needed to explore light and shadow properly. A light box placed in a darker part

Objects on a light box encourage exploration and investigation

of the room will draw children in to look closely at natural and transparent objects placed on it. They can investigate pattern and colour and explore what things are made of and how they behave.

Light from an overhead projector placed on a low table, or on the floor, can be projected onto a plain wall, a sheet, the ceiling or the floor. Objects placed on the projector screen create dark, pale or coloured shadows and can be moved around to create large pictures, patterns and stories. These all provide interesting starting points for conversations and discussions and opportunities for small groups of children to play together cooperatively.

Reflection

Mirrors are an endless source of fascination for young children as they invite self-discovery and promote self-awareness. Reflective or mirrored

Mirrors placed just above floor level encourage young babies
to investigate their reflections

surfaces can be created in many different ways. Mirror tables, mirror exploratories and 'infinity boxes' can be placed in different parts of the room to present resources to the children in new and different ways. This will prompt children's curiosity and encourage them to explore and investigate. Mirrored surfaces at child height – along the walls, on the sides of furniture units and as free-standing mirrors – all engage children's attention and help them to see the world from different angles and viewpoints. Children will catch sight of themselves and their friends while playing, and will spend long periods of time interacting with their reflections. In this way they become very familiar with the way in which reflected images move, supporting their mathematical understanding of position, shape, space and measure.

Reflective surfaces placed at angles to one another, for example in a kaleidoscope or triptych mirror, create interesting 'mirrored dens' for children to explore and investigate. The multiple images and interesting effects produced by the reflections act as wonderful starting points to stimulate children's imagination and support their language development.

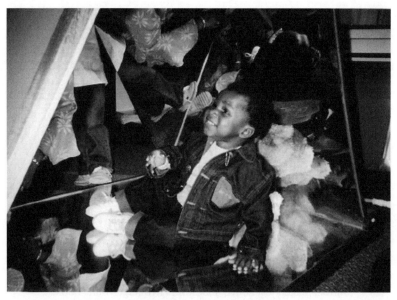

Multiple reflections in a kaleidoscope mirror invoke surprise and delight

For safety reasons acrylic safety mirror is used in place of glass in the UK. High-quality acrylic provides a good reflection, but can be damaged by scratching so it is important to think about the resources you provide for the children to use in mirrored equipment, and to use perspex protective covers wherever possible.

Out of doors, shiny objects create reflections and can give unusual and interesting glimpses of the sky and the clouds. The surface of a puddle will also act as a reflective surface if it is very smooth and still.

Multi-sensory spaces

Often we use our sense of sight to gather information about what our environment is like – we tend to focus on what it looks like. It is important to remember that young children, and particularly babies, will also be using their other senses – hearing, smell and touch – to explore the space they are in. Planning a multi-sensory environment will give children lots of opportunities to develop their whole range of sensory awareness.

Remember to consider the environment from the perspective of very young children. They are much closer to floor level than we are as adults and how they 'see' the setting when they look around varies with how old they are. Babies in particular will have a great interest in the floor, the skirting boards and the ceiling. Try crawling around your setting and looking out of the windows to get an impression of what it is like. What does it feel like? What does it smell like? What does it sound like? What does it look like?

Textures

Different textures and materials used as floor coverings and on walls and doors will give children lots of sensory opportunities and, as they become older, will help to develop their vocabulary and language. Consider how you could use carpet, lino, tiles, slate, AstroTurf, brick, stone, wood, metal, fabric, mirrors and perspex in ways which encourage children to become familiar with these different materials – what they feel like, what they smell like and what they sound like.

Colour

Think about how you use colour in your setting. We have a tendency in the UK to use lots of strong vibrant colours in environments for young children. Toys and equipment for young children are often brightly coloured as well, as are children's clothes. This can lead to a confusion of colour in a room, making it hard to pick out individual items. Rugs and table coverings with complicated bright patterns on them can make it very difficult for children to focus their attention on the resources they are playing with. Pastel colours can help to create a calm and peaceful environment. Paler colours on walls, ceilings and floors and plain table covers will provide a neutral backdrop and resources, displays and equipment will stand out better.

Sound

Creating 'quiet spaces' within busy early years settings can sometimes be challenging. Children need to have restful quiet spaces they can escape to where they can relax, talk quietly, look at books and think. This could be a semi-permanent feature in one part of the room, with a canopy, rugs and floor cushions, or a temporary space created by the children as a den.

Music can be used very effectively to create a 'mood' within a room. Children will respond differently to quiet calm music and loud vibrant music – try playing different music in the background while children are drawing or painting and observe how this affects the artwork that they produce.

Smell

There are lots of different ways in which we can develop children's awareness of their sense of smell. These include bringing into the setting scented flowers and plants, pot-pourri, and strongly scented wood such as cedar and freshly cut pine. By simply encouraging children to smell everyday things as well as looking and touching, we can make them more aware of their sense of smell. Meal times are ideal opportunities during the day to encourage children to focus on smell, and to try to guess what something is by what it smells like.

Outdoors

The outdoor environment of your setting is an ideal place to encourage children's awareness of smells and sounds. A sensory garden with herbs and other strongly scented plants can be created in a corner of your outdoor area, or in a large container or tub. Brushing against the leaves releases their scent so think about placing some plants where the children will touch them as they play. Wind chimes, placed so they catch the breeze, can produce a variety of different sounds depending on the material they are made of – metal, plastic, bamboo or shells, for example. Encourage children to listen carefully to sounds outdoors and to try to identify different things in their environment from the sounds that they make.

Snapshots

Thinking about the importance of the environment and how you might improve it is an essential step towards bringing the Reggio Approach to your early years setting. The practical ideas in this chapter will help you begin. The following snapshots of good practice show how two early years settings have been influenced by Reggio's approach to the environment.

An environment for babies and toddlers

The manager of a newly opened children's centre was inspired by a visit to Reggio Emilia and wanted to create an environment which would be attractive for the youngest children in the centre, parents and staff. Some areas of the building were to be rebuilt and others were changed by thinking imaginatively.

The 'meeters and greeters' table

The entrance to the children's centre is a welcoming place which invites the visitor in. It has photographs of children busy with activities, a display showing all members of staff and their roles in the centre, and a plan for parents and visitors to help them find their way around. Low windows in the toddler room overlook the path to the entrance and new arrivals can be seen by the young 'meeters and greeters' inside the building.

Outdoor clothes and shoes are stored in lockers inside each of the home bases. This encourages parents to enter the building and to engage in conversation with their child's key person, rather than 'dropping off' their children at the entrance.

The rooms for babies and toddlers appeal to all the senses. Different textures are found on the floors and walls, mirrors are used so that children can see things from different angles and there are small, curtained spaces to play peekaboo or to hide in. Sleeping areas include wicker 'nests' which the children can climb in and out of independently. Ceilings have soft drapes and canopies made from transparent fabrics, and dimmer switches, torches and a light box give different levels of light. In the bathrooms and changing areas multi-sensory experiences come from a variety of scents, textures, mirrors and music.

Ben's Bistro

A nursery decided to focus on how it could improve the environment at meal times by developing a 'bistro' with the older children. The staff began by talking to the children about cafes they had visited and what they liked about them. They talked about how the tables and chairs are set out, the decorations, the way tables are laid, how the food is served and how 'customers' are expected to behave. It was decided that the bistro needed to be special – a beautiful place where children could be with their friends and serve the food themselves.

After much discussion with the children, meal times in this nursery are now very different.

In the half hour before lunch three or four of the children – this week's lunchtime waiters – begin to transform their home base into 'Ben's Bistro'. The rest of the group listen to a story in the next room and begin to get ready for lunch. In the bistro, tables and chairs are moved into groupings of six or eight places and covered with table-cloths. Each table is decorated with a vase of flowers or a small plant and a menu setting out the choices for the day.

The waiters set places for six or eight people at each table using place mats, serviettes, china plates and bowls, real cutlery and glass tumblers. This is a perfect opportunity for children to count, match, order and sort in a 'real life' situation. When all the arrangements are complete one of the waiters makes a final check to make sure that everything is in place and that the bistro is ready to open for guests.

The rest of the children are then invited into the bistro for lunch. The food is brought to each table in serving dishes and the children are encouraged to serve themselves and to help one another. Adults sit with the children during the meal. Over lunch, the adults and children talk together about things that have happened during the morning or about what is happening in the children's lives at home.

Meal times are now relaxed, social occasions with plenty of time to eat, talk and enjoy the company of friends. At the end of the meal the waiters help to clear the tables and tidy up and reorganise the room, ready for the start of the afternoon session.

Practitioners point out that changing the environment in this way on a daily basis requires planning and organisation as well as a shared understanding among staff of the importance of meal times.

Further reading

Ceppi, G. and Zini, M. (eds) (1998) *Children, Spaces, Relations: Metaproject for an Environment for Young Children*. Italy: Reggio Children.

This book describes a research project carried out in Reggio Emilia by architects, engineers, designers and educators. The research looked closely at the relationship between the pedagogy of the Reggio Approach and the architecture of the infant-toddler centre and preschool buildings. In the book the authors describe how the physical environment can be a partner in the learning process for young children.

Questions to think about

Every space has a purpose

- Walk around your setting – does every space have a purpose?
- Is it clear why each space is arranged the way it is?
- Do we know which spaces children, staff and parents like or dislike?
- Are there some spaces we would like to change?

The environment as the third teacher

- Does our environment help or hinder what we want to do?

- How often do we change the layout of our room?

- Do we make use of light, shadow and reflection?

- Do children have lots of opportunities to experience textures, smells and sounds?

Inside and outside

- How flexible can we be in giving children access to the outdoors?

- Do we make good use of learning opportunities outdoors, and in all weathers?

- How do we make the most of the natural world?

- Can we bring 'the outside in', or take 'the indoors out'?

5 | Time

In the Reggio Approach

Valuing time

Time is valued in the Reggio Approach for all the different opportunities it provides. In particular, educators in Reggio value time for:

- **continuity** – children and teachers build up strong relationships as they stay together for the whole three-year period that children attend the centre;
- **daily life** – time to be, to do, to meet, to play, to think and reflect, to talk, to listen, to rest and to eat;
- **long-term projects** – known in Reggio as 'progettazione', which last from a few days to three months.

Time for continuity

The Reggio Approach values the phase from birth to 6 years of age as a stage in its own right, not simply as a preparation for the future. Teachers and parents in Reggio do not talk about 'getting children ready for school'. Instead they value giving children time to experience the joy of being 1 or 3 or 5 years old.

Pictures and stories from projects which have happened in the past are part of the environment of the school, indoors and out. There are drawings, photographs, descriptions and models in the classrooms, the atelier, the entrance hall, the piazza and the garden. These traces of children who have gone before help the current children to see that they are part of a much larger community. Keeping and displaying young children's work in this way also gives children very powerful messages about how important the adults think their learning is.

Time during the day

The preschool and infant-toddler centre day is planned so that children can spend long periods of uninterrupted time on activities which interest them. If a particular experience engages their attention they are able to revisit it many times to consolidate their understanding.

Organisation of the day

There are only three fixed times in the day – the start of the morning session, lunchtime and the time when children leave. This allows children to be involved in activities for long periods of time.

A typical day in an infant-toddler centre

7.30–9.00	Children arrive
9.00–11.00	Morning session
11.00–12.00	Lunch in the dining room
12.00–1.00	Quiet activities, preparation for sleep and mid-day departure
1.00–2.45	Afternoon sleep and quiet play
2.45	Afternoon snack
3.00–3.30	Reflecting on the day and preparing for departure
3.30–4.00	Children leave
4.00–6.20	Extended day for parents who need the service.

A typical day in a preschool

7.30–9.00	Children arrive; child-initiated activities
9.00–11.30	Large group session followed by play and organised work activities in large and small groups
11.30–12.00	Coming together and sharing the morning's experiences
12.00–1.00	Lunch in the dining room
1.00–3.00	Afternoon nap and quiet activities
3.00	Snack in the classroom
3.30–4.00	Children leave
4.00–6.20	Extended day for parents who need the service.

Time for long-term projects

Anyone who has seen The Hundred Languages of Children exhibition will be aware of the large-scale, long-term projects which young children in Reggio are involved in. Some of these projects may last only a few weeks, others go on for up to three months. Occasionally a large-scale project, such as 'Reggio Tutta' ('All About Reggio'), can last up to two years. This project looked at the children's views and feelings about living in the city of Reggio Emilia and it involved the whole network of infant-toddler centres and preschools.

A starting point for projects can come from children's interests and questions, events that have happened in the centre or ideas that the adults suggest and the children are keen to follow up on. In the early stages of a project a lot of time is spent by teachers and children talking about different possibilities and investigating different ideas. The final choice for a project comes out of this discussion, but at this stage the final product and how long it will last have not been decided.

A small group of children who are particularly enthusiastic about the idea take on responsibility for the project. Work on the project happens in the classroom, in the atelier or in the mini atelier on a daily basis for as long as is necessary. At the beginning of each morning session there is a class assembly where children agree what they are going to do for the morning, where they are going to do it, and who they are going to work with. A group of children involved in a project will then work together on some aspect of it for part of the morning session. In the half hour before lunch the children come together again as a class and share what they have been doing during the morning. This helps to keep the whole class connected with the progress of a project and gives them a chance to offer their own ideas and observations. Projects end when teachers and children decide to move on to a new topic of interest.

In the Reggio Approach it is always the learning process, not the final product, which is important.

Quality practice in the Early Years Foundation Stage

In Reggio, planning the structure of the day around three fixed points – arrival time, lunchtime and home time – creates a flexible routine in which children have time to explore their interests and spend uninterrupted periods of time on things which engage their curiosity. Long-term projects enable children to revisit activities again and again and learning environments are organised so that 'work in progress' can be left out from one day to the next.

The revised EYFS framework highlights the importance of providing time for children to follow their interests and consolidate their learning, recognising that every child is a unique child, who is constantly learning and can be resilient, capable, confident and self-assured. This is also highlighted in the definition of active learning which, along with playing and exploring and creating and thinking critically, is one of the three characteristics of effective learning.

Active learning

As a description of how young children learn, active learning focuses on the attitudes and dispositions that describe children's motivation. It includes three key characteristics: being involved and concentrating, keeping on trying and enjoying achieving.

- *Being involved and concentrating* describes the intensity of attention that children show when they concentrate on ideas and activities which interest them. Children need time and opportunity to become fully engrossed in their play and there is evidence to show that high levels of concentration and involvement lead to 'deep level learning'.

- *Keeping on trying* highlights the importance of children persisting in the face of challenges or difficulties, thereby becoming more resilient. To do this it is important that children have time to become engaged with activities that interest them and that they are able to return to activities again and again until their curiosity is satisfied.

- Children *enjoying achieving what they set out to do* refers to the reward they feel when they meet their own goals. Having time to learn how to do something for oneself builds the intrinsic moti-vation which supports long-term success.

Inspiration from the Reggio Approach

Making the most of time

Thinking about all the different things which happen during the day and seeing the value each can bring to young children's learning and devel-opment will help you to make the most of the time children spend with you in your setting. During the course of the day children need time to:

- play, explore and investigate;

- communicate with one another and with adults;

- think and reflect;

- eat and drink;

- rest and sleep;

- be outdoors;

- be involved in long-term projects.

Planning a daily routine which works well for both adults and children depends on achieving a balance between the organisational needs of the adults and the interests and needs of the children. In any well-organised setting certain events have to take place at specific times of the day, but within this framework it is possible to adopt a flexible approach which also makes the most of the many learning opportunities which arise from everyday routines.

Time to play, explore and investigate

For children to develop their interests and extend their learning they need opportunities to become engrossed with ideas and activities which interest them. Organising your daily routine to give children uninterrupted time, and planning the environment so that they can have the opportunity to come back to activities again and again will help to develop children's skills of concentration, persistence and diligence.

In Reggio, babies and young children spend a great deal of time exploring natural and reclaimed materials, light, shadow, colour and reflection (see Chapters 3 and 4). Open-ended materials and resources are provided on a daily basis for children to use as starting points for investigations. Alongside these, rooms are equipped with light boxes, overhead projectors, mirrors and shadow screens to encourage children to observe carefully, experiment and use their imagination.

Time to communicate

A 'whole group time' at the beginning of the morning when children gather together to discuss what they are going to do during the day is an ideal occasion to develop speaking and listening skills. This is an opportunity to share with children the ideas and activities which have been planned for the day and gather their input into what might happen. It gives children the opportunity to think about all the different possibilities on offer and helps them to make informed choices.

During these group sessions children can put forward ideas about what they want to do, where they would like to be and who they want to work with. These provide ideal opportunities to practise the skills of negotiation and cooperation and help children to learn some simple time management skills.

Gathering together again as a group before lunchtime draws the morning session to a close and is a time for children to share with others what they have discovered during the morning. Children can practise the communication skills needed to explain their ideas and observations and can learn how to listen to the contributions of others. Plans can also be made for how time will be spent during the afternoon session.

Time to think and reflect

To consolidate their understanding children need time and regular opportunities to reflect on what they are doing and think about what they have learned. Reflective practitioners can support this process by valuing this 'thinking time' and by creating opportunities during the day when children are encouraged to stand back and think about what has happened. Photographs of children involved in activities, and tape recordings of children's conversations are ideal prompts to encourage this type of discussion.

Time to eat and drink

Regular meal and snack times and free access to drinking water are an important part of the daily routine of any early years setting. Snack time during the morning can be arranged over a period of half to three-quarters of an hour, with children having their mid-morning snack together in small groups. This again provides an ideal opportunity for focused conversation about what children have been doing, for practising the skills of pouring drinks and cutting fruit and for appreciating the importance of being polite and helpful to one another.

By recognising all the important social learning opportunities which exist around meal times, lunchtime can become a highlight of the day, and an important social occasion, rather than a chore to be got over with as quickly as possible (see 'Ben's Bistro' p. 65). Children can help to prepare the room and the tables for meal times, developing their mathematical understanding as they do so. Lunchtime becomes a time for practising a wide range of social and physical skills as well as an opportunity for trying out new things.

Time to rest and sleep

Rest and sleep make a vital contribution to a healthy lifestyle for young children. Tired children are irritable, unable to concentrate and unlikely to benefit from the learning opportunities on offer to them. Time and space for children to rest quietly and to sleep is an essential feature of an early years setting. The time when children are resting is an ideal opportunity for practitioners to write up observations made during the morning session. It is also a good time to think about the kinds of experiences it would be appropriate to offer children next in order to move their learning on.

Time to be outdoors

It is well recognised that children benefit from the opportunity to play, explore and investigate outside for at least part of the day, whatever the weather. The outdoors offers opportunities to:

- move around freely, to run, jump, dance and perform;
- build and construct on a grand scale;
- experience the weather and the seasons;
- observe the movement of shadows and the passage of time;
- explore all the interesting and unusual features of the natural and the built environment.

Managing time outdoors will depend on the design of your building, the nature of your outdoor space and the organisational structure of your setting. Time spent outdoors is as effective and useful in supporting young children's learning as time spent indoors. Indeed, for some children it will be more effective. Being flexible and open-minded in timetabling the use of your outdoor space is essential.

Time to be involved in long-term projects

Planning longer-term projects to carry out with children is an ideal way of capitalising on children's interests and curiosity while at the same time providing meaningful opportunities to extend their skills, knowledge and understanding.

Starting points for projects may come from:

- ideas the children have while they are investigating and exploring;

- situations or events which arise 'spontaneously' in the setting;

- suggestions which you as practitioners make and then discuss with the children;

- ideas put forward by colleagues, parents or members of the local community.

When planning a long-term project it is important to be as open-minded and flexible about the final outcome as possible. Remember it is the learning which children experience during the process of the project that is important, not the final outcome or product. Children's long-term interest and involvement in the project will be maintained if they can see that their ideas are being taken seriously and are shaping the progress of the project.

As a project develops children need regular opportunities to remember how the work they are currently involved in relates to things that have happened in the past. Plan time into your weekly schedule to do this and use photographs, drawings, pictures and records of conversations to act as prompts to help children to remember.

The time and effort invested in carrying out a long-term project will result in a product which everyone – adults and children – feels proud of. Rather than consigning this to a cupboard at the end of the year, you may like to think about finding a way of making it a long-term feature of your setting. This will bring a sense of history to your setting which will be obvious to new parents and children and to new recruits to the staff team.

Snapshot

This snapshot describes a long-term project which was inspired by the Reggio Approach, but which is firmly rooted in the culture of the local community.

The enchanted garden

Children and staff of a nursery school in north-west England worked with an artist and an engineer on a long-term project which resulted in an installation to enhance the nursery garden.

One of the bird sculptures made during the Enchanted Garden project

During this period the adults talked to the children about their experiences and waited for a theme to arise. Out of this process came the theme for the project – blue trees for the birds to perch on.

Children's experience of birds was then enhanced by providing books, pictures and artefacts around the setting to act as starting points for children's creative expression.

The final outcomes, and the title of the project, were not decided before the project began. Instead a starting point was chosen – in this case a visit to the local botanic gardens – and children were encouraged to experience many different aspects of the natural environment.

The blue bird tree installed in the nursery garden

Back in the nursery, time was spent discussing the visit – children investigated the leaves, branches, seeds and pods they had brought back with them and made paintings and drawings.

Children spent time expressing their ideas in many different forms – drawing and painting pictures of birds, making model birds in clay, creating shadow puppets and acting out their ideas about birds through movement and performance.

Time and care was taken to provide the materials and resources children needed, including the human resources of creative adults. Children spent time practising the woodworking skills they needed to design and make birds out of wood.

As the project progressed the small group of children who were most closely involved in creating the bird sculptures were given time to report back regularly to the rest of the group, keeping them closely involved with development of the project.

Finally, time was set aside to celebrate the installation of the final construction, with the bird tree now a permanent feature of the nursery grounds.

Throughout the process adults spent time on documenting the children's learning using photographs, video and tape recordings of conversations.

Further reading

Vecchi, V. (ed.) (2002) *Theater Curtain: The Ring of Transformations.* Italy: Reggio Children.

A beautifully illustrated description of the project carried out by children from the Diana school which led to the production of the safety curtain for the Ariosto Theatre. A detailed description of a long-term project.

Giudici, C., Rinaldi, C. and Krechevsky, M. (eds) (2001) *Making Learning Visible: Children as Individual and Group Learners.* Italy: Reggio Children.

A joint publication with Project Zero at Harvard University in America. This looks at the learning of children and adults in groups and gives very detailed examples of daily life in a preschool and infant-toddler centre. It is an ideal text for supporting continuous professional development.

Questions to think about

The pattern of the day

- How do we decide what the pattern of the day in our setting should be?

- Do we give children enough uninterrupted time to become involved in activities that interest them?

- Can children return to 'work in progress' later in the day/week?

- Are our routines flexible enough to allow children to follow their interests?

Time for children to think and reflect

- Do we encourage children to spend time thinking about what they have done?

- How do we help them to remember things that have happened?

- Is time for discussion and conversation valued?

- Do we spend time helping children to refine their ideas and consolidate their learning?

Time for long-term projects

- Do we spend enough time on planning and carrying out long-term projects?

- How do we help children stay connected with a project over a long period of time?

- Do we give children time to develop their skills and understanding?

- How well do we enable children to manage their own time?

6 | Learning and teaching

In the Reggio Approach

Children and teachers learning together

Research is at the heart of the Reggio experience and the Reggio Approach is constantly evolving as teachers learn more about how young children learn.

In Reggio the adults in the infant-toddler centre and preschools believe that the role of the teacher is not just to teach, but to learn. The teachers learn from one another, from the atelierista and the pedagogista. They also learn from the children with whom they share experiences and ideas on a daily basis. Being comfortable about seeing children as partners in teaching and learning links back to the very powerful image they have of the child in the Reggio Approach (*see* Chapter 2).

Children are encouraged to think of themselves as researchers, developing their own understanding of the world. They do this from their own experiences and from sharing the experiences of the other members of their group, class or school – adults as well as children. There are times during each day when children meet together to share experiences and review events. The teachers help children to remember what has happened and to develop the habit of reflecting on their previous experiences. Working in this way helps children to see themselves as very clearly connected to the other children and adults in their school.

The curriculum framework

In the Reggio Approach, children and teachers do not follow a set formal curriculum. Instead, children's questions and ideas are used as starting points for developing their learning and teachers use their skills and experience to build on these foundations. Children and adults explore ideas together, learning from one another and building their knowledge and understanding together.

There is, however, a framework of 'progettazione' or 'projects' which underpins the way teachers and children work together in Reggio. This curriculum framework is based on the belief that:

- knowledge building is not linear or predetermined in advance;

- the development of knowledge is a group process;

- children produce their own theories and have their own values.

It is possible to divide the types of progettazione into four groups:

1. **Themed projects** which cover four areas of learning which all children will encounter each year. These are:

   ○ relationships with oneself and others;

   ○ colour theory;

   ○ communication and representation;

   ○ books.

2. **Environmental projects** which arise out of the core experiences, resources and equipment available in the classroom, such as the construction area, the light box, mirrors, message boxes, role-play and book areas.

3. **Daily life projects** which come from the daily assembly or daily life at school. These projects might include:

   ○ the journey to school or arrival and departure;

○ meal times;

○ out of doors;

○ negotiation, forming groups and conflict resolution.

4. **Self-managed projects** which are set up for children to do independently – individually or as part of a small group. These might be wire sculptures, weaving or mandala pictures and patterns made from natural or reclaimed materials without the use of glue.

Aspects of progettazione

Most of the projects in Reggio follow a similar pattern. All of the aspects of progettazione listed below will be in place – making them more than simply 'projects' as we know them in the UK.

1. Provocations, questions and wait time.

A provocation is introduced to the children – this is a stimulus or thought provoker which invites wonder, curiosity and investigation. This could be, for example, a photograph of the sunset, a giant leaf or a striped snail shell. Children and adults will ask questions and then a period of waiting may occur to enable the children to come up with their ideas and theories.

2. Developing the project idea and giving the project a name. The progettazione have very carefully chosen names, many of them chosen by the children themselves. For example, 'Everything has a shadow except ants', 'My nose is as full as a world', 'The monument to colour' or 'Horses in love'.

3. Carrying out the project.

4. Documenting the project. Of course, the documentation of the project will happen from the beginning.

Group learning

Group learning is very highly valued in the Reggio Approach. A great deal of emphasis is placed on helping children to share their experiences and learn from one another. Time is planned during the day to create many opportunities for children to work together in small groups. In a learning group children are encouraged to express their ideas and to listen to the ideas of others. In this way they learn the skills of negotiation and cooperation and how to play a part as a member of a team.

Children spend a lot of time representing their ideas and theories about the world and how it works. The word 'represent' is thought of as 're-present' where ideas are expressed first in words, then in drawings, 3-D models and, sometimes, through movement. The children are encouraged to talk about what their pictures show and to explain their drawings and models to the other members of their group. As they 're-present' their thoughts in different ways they begin to understand their own ideas more clearly, and to develop their critical thinking skills.

Documentation

Documentation describes the process which teachers in Reggio use to help them understand young children's thinking and learning. In the Reggio Approach documentation is used as a way of making children's learning visible to the children themselves, to teachers and to parents.

Documentation involves **observation**. In this context observation means not just looking at what children are doing, but listening to what they are saying and tuning in to the many different 'languages of expression' which children use.

Different tools of observation are used for different age groups of children and in different learning situations. These can include photos, video, written notes, tape recordings as well as the children's drawings and models.

With babies and very young children observation focuses on seeing and noting their actions and body language. This includes the movements, gestures and sounds that they make and the way in which they approach different situations, resources and people.

As children get older there is more emphasis on recording the words the children use. When children are busy with an activity the teacher often takes photographs to record the learning which is going on. These photographs are always accompanied by written notes which capture the exact words the children were using in their conversations. This pairing up of words and pictures gives the teacher a much clearer picture of the children's thoughts and ideas.

Documentation also involves **interpretation**. Sharing observations with others helps teachers to gain different viewpoints on what is actually happening in any learning situation.

Teachers in the infant-toddler centres and preschools share their observations every day. They talk together about what they have seen and heard and help one another to interpret what children are learning in different situations. They then use this information to plan what to do next with the children.

The uses of documentation

In Reggio, documentation is used to:

- record progress and development by helping teachers to see and understand the learning of individual children, as well as recognising the contribution they make to the learning of the whole group;

- value children's ideas by paying attention to the way children's work is presented and shared;

- encourage children to reflect by giving them the opportunity to revisit their earlier experiences and develop their understanding of their own learning processes;

- help with planning by suggesting to teachers which resources, experiences or skills to offer children next;

- involve parents by providing information about the life of the centres, helping them to understand more about their child's learning;

- add to teachers' professional development by producing evidence which can be reviewed, discussed and reinterpreted with colleagues and the pedagogical advisory team;

- celebrate the life and work of the centres by taking children's work out of the centres into the public buildings, streets and shops of the city of Reggio Emilia and around the world in The Hundred Languages of Children exhibition.

Quality practice in the Early Years Foundation Stage

In Reggio, teachers and children build their knowledge, understanding and skills together – they are co-constructors of knowledge. The teachers see the value in building their curriculum framework around the interests of the children and the questions and ideas they present. While the adults are careful to recognise individual learning preferences, individual needs and forms of expression, they acknowledge group learning as highly important in their approach.

In the revised EYFS framework practitioners must consider the individual needs, interests, and stage of development of each child in their care, and must use this information to plan a challenging and enjoyable experience for each child in all of the areas of learning and development. Each area of learning and development must be implemented through planned, purposeful play and through a mix of adult-led and child-initiated activity. Play is seen as essential for children's development, building their confidence as they learn to explore, to think about problems, and relate to others. Children learn by leading their own play, and by taking part in play which is guided by adults. There is an ongoing judgement to be made by practitioners about the balance between activities led by children, and activities led or guided by adults.

The revised EYFS contains seven areas of learning. The three prime areas are:

- communication and language;

- physical development;

- personal, social and emotional development.

And the four specific areas:

- literacy;

- mathematics;

- understanding of the world;

- expressive arts and design.

Practitioners working with the youngest children are expected to focus strongly on the three prime areas, which are the basis for successful learning in the other four specific areas. The three prime areas reflect the key skills and capacities all children need to develop and learn effectively, and become ready for school. There is an expectation that the balance will shift towards a more equal focus on all areas of learning as children grow in confidence and ability within the three prime areas.

In addition, practitioners need to be aware of the three characteristics of effective learning, play and exploration, active learning, and creating and thinking critically which reflect how young children approach their learning.

- Playing and exploring focuses on how children investigate and experience things, and 'have a go'.

- Active learning highlights how children concentrate and keep on trying if they encounter difficulties, and how they enjoy achievements.

- Creating and thinking critically recognises that children have and develop their own ideas, make links between ideas, and develop strategies for doing things.

Effective learning for young children

Effective learning for young children involves:

- children feeling safe and secure, which helps them to become confident learners;
- children initiating activities which promote learning and enable them to learn from each other;
- children learning through movement and all their senses;
- children having time to explore interests and ideas in depth;
- children learning in different ways and at different rates;
- children making links in their learning – making links in learning is the basis of creativity and becoming an effective learner;
- creative and imaginative play activities that promote the development and use of language.

Effective teaching

Teaching means systematically helping children to learn so that they are helped to make connections in their learning and are actively led forward as well as helped to reflect on what they have already learned. Teaching has many aspects including:

- planning and creating a learning environment;
- organising time and material resources;
- interacting, questioning, responding to questions;
- assessing and recording children's progress and sharing knowledge gained with other practitioners and parents.

Effective teaching includes:

- working in partnership with parents;

- promoting children's learning through planned experiences that are challenging but achievable;

- practitioners who model a positive behaviour;

- using language that is rich and using correct grammar;

- using conversation and carefully framed questions because this is crucial in developing children's knowledge;

- direct teaching of skills and knowledge;

- children teaching each other;

- interacting with, and supporting, children in a way that positively affects the attitudes to learning that children develop;

- planning the indoor and outdoor environment carefully to provide a positive context for learning and teaching;

- using assessment to evaluate the quality of provision and practitioners' training needs.

Inspiration from the Reggio Approach

The Hundred Languages of Children exhibition, which toured the UK in 2000 and 2004–05, inspired tens of thousands of practitioners in the UK. The beautifully documented panels from the infant-toddler centres and preschools of Reggio Emilia demonstrated the quality of the learning and teaching which takes place on a daily basis.

Many of those who saw the exhibition, along with those who have visited the infant-toddler centres and preschools themselves, have reviewed the teaching and learning in their own settings. The areas they have looked at include:

- developing children's ideas and theories;

- planning open-ended projects;

- individual and group learning;
- documentation;
- sharing learning with parents;
- celebrating learning.

Developing children's ideas and theories

Children are naturally curious from the day they are born. They very soon begin to develop ideas and theories about the world around them, even before they can express their ideas in words. Adults in your setting need to engage with children on an individual basis, encouraging them to express their ideas and feelings and listening to what they have to say.

Having good conversations with children does not happen by chance. As staff you need to plan opportunities to have good conversations – choose a comfortable place, make sure you allow plenty of time, be prepared to listen not talk. Decide in advance how you are going to record both the conversations you have with children and those they have with their group.

Use a tape recorder to record children's discussions. This can then be played back to the children at a later date, to remind them of what they had to say and the good ideas they had. Remember that young children do not have the ability to take notes to remind them of what they said, thought and heard.

In order to develop children's ideas and theories you need to provide a climate where children are confident to ask questions, seek explanations and develop their critical thinking and problem-solving skills. To encourage children to ask questions you will need to:

- provide them with lots of opportunities;
- show, by your words and your body language, that you value their answers;

- give children time to think and respond to questions you ask – don't be tempted to fill the silences;

- listen to children's answers before asking the next question;

- be a role model by thinking out loud, asking yourself questions such as, 'I wonder why…?', 'What would happen if…?'

The sorts of questions which you will find useful in developing children's ideas and theories include:

- questions which follow the children's interests and ideas;

- questions which have more than one possible answer and which encourage further investigation;

- real questions to which you do not know the answer yourself. These questions will encourage shared ideas, explorations and discoveries.

Giving children the opportunity to express their ideas in a variety of forms – in words, in pictures, in 3-D models – will help them to refine their thinking and to experience deep-level learning.

Don't forget that you will need to provide interesting objects and experiences to stimulate children's ideas and theories – like all of us, they need something to think about which captures their interest and motivation.

Planning open-ended topics

Often it can be easier for a practitioner to have a set idea of what it is the children ought to learn, and a focused set of activities to make this happen. It is essential that any planning system you use leaves room for the unexpected, for spontaneity and for time to follow individual interests in depth.

Using titles for projects which do not limit the scope of potential learning will make it easier to involve the children in deciding, and planning, what they want to learn. Many practitioners have begun to move away from specific project titles such as 'People who help us' or 'My body' to open-ended projects such as 'Let's imagine', 'Stories', or 'Under a stone'. Projects such as 'Light, shadow and reflection' can be built around equipment and resources in your setting. Daily routines can lead to projects such as 'Journeys' or 'What can I do to help you?'

Quite rightly, practitioners are expected to be aware of the learning objectives of the experiences they provide for young children and to plan accordingly. What is important is that there is a balance between learning objectives which are decided by the adult/s and those which follow the children's interests, building on what they already know. Try using the term 'Emergent objectives' (Thornton and Brunton 2004) for a section within your planning format. This will allow you to include the learning objectives, questions and ideas raised by the children alongside those areas of learning which you have decided to plan for in advance.

Individual and group learning

Individual learning

As adults, we all have preferred ways of learning. Some of us prefer to see, rather than hear, information. Some of us prefer to read about something, others need to really do it! Children are no different and they will show their preferred ways of learning from an early age. Practitioners need to be able to respond to children's different learning preferences, providing them with experiences which will encourage their individual learning.

Children will also choose to express themselves in different ways, showing what they have learned, what they have understood and what skills they have acquired. Be prepared to value the learning of the child who expresses himself through performance, music or physical play as well as the child who prefers to draw, 'write' or role play.

The important thing is for **all** practitioners to recognise **all** children as individual learners with a wide range of learning preferences and forms of expression.

Group learning

In Reggio Emilia the educators focus on group learning in their early childhood centres. Many early years practitioners in the UK are developing ways to encourage genuine group learning for even the youngest children.

A good way to introduce group learning is to set the group a challenge or a problem to solve, such as organising a visit to the local park for a picnic, or making a giant sundial for the outside area of your setting. The ideas and theories which come out of the challenge you set will help you to plan for the next stage in the children's learning.

When you plan for group learning to take place remember that:

- both adults and children are members of the learning group – and the adult is not always in charge;

- children will learn to collaborate, work as part of a team and negotiate;

- as the adult, you may need to ensure that the group sets rules for itself and sticks to them;

- children and adults together will develop critical thinking skills and become emotionally involved in the work of the group;

- discoveries made by individual children will become part of the learning of all of the members of the group.

Documentation

One of the greatest influences that the Reggio Approach has had on early years practice in the UK is the quality of documentation found in many early years settings.

We have a long tradition of displaying children's work but there has often been a focus on displaying the final product, not the learning process.

Increasingly, many early years settings use documentation to show how:

- children acquire knowledge;
- children organise and process knowledge;
- children carry out research.

Documentation is being used to show how:

- practitioners listen to children;
- practitioners increase their knowledge with, and about, children;
- practitioners value children and their ways of learning.

Observations of children are being enriched by practitioners who:

- are sensitive to children's different forms of expression;
- observe using all their senses, not just sight;
- actively listen to children, recording the actual words that children say – this is how we find out what children are thinking and learning.

You can use many different tools to record observations – photographs and videos, tape recordings, notes, sketches and written transcripts. The children's drawings and paintings and 3-D models will all contribute to your observations of how children think and learn.

Instead of observing only what children are doing, you can focus on their conversations and discussions, their interactions and relationships, the way they use all their senses to explore the world around them. When observing babies and toddlers, look carefully at their gestures, stance and posture as these are all indicators of their interest, motivation and learning.

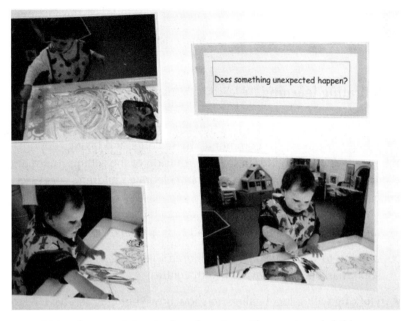

Using documentation to share learning with parents and children

Sharing learning with parents

Most early years settings in the UK have systems for sharing children's development and daily activities with individual parents, often in the form of learning journeys/journals. Although there is still a strong tradition of 'having something to take home' at the end of each session, you could make sharing children's learning with parents more inter-active and interesting by:

- a daily diary for the whole group using digital photographs and observations;

- displaying documentation (photographs, the children's words and your observations) which shows the learning process rather than the end product;

- an automatic PowerPoint presentation of the children in the entrance;
- well presented booklets for parents, created at the end of a project.

Celebrating learning

More and more early years practitioners are recognising the value of engaging with the local community by making, and taking, opportunities to celebrate children's learning outside of the setting. There are many different ways in which you can celebrate children's successes, such as:

- taking part in local festivals, parades or special events;
- offering to create displays of children's learning in local libraries, supermarkets, museums or health centres;
- working with a local gallery to show how your children have been inspired by art work and photography;
- developing a partnership with a local theatre or drama group to put on a performance;
- persuading your local authority to develop a longer-term project with your setting – perhaps around recycling or a child's guide to your area;
- inviting the local community in to see your documentation of the children's, and, of course, your own, learning.

Snapshot

The following snapshot describes how a practitioner in a daycare nursery researched how an individual child's creative expression was influenced by interacting with other children in a group situation. She used her skills of documentation to record the group of children's conversations, ideas and interactions.

Making maps together

A group of 3- and 4-year-old children, accompanied by adults, had visited a local pet shop and taken photographs to record the route they had taken. These pictures became the subject of discussion at 'circle time' when a small group of children decided to make drawings of their journey.

The children were offered large pieces of paper with a pencil outline of the roads that they had gone down, with the intention that they might then add drawings of the places that interested them, or that had been recorded in photographs.

The children worked enthusiastically on their individual maps, but all did not follow the original preconceived plan. The oldest boy in the group had been on holiday to India at the time of the pet shop trip so, instead, he drew the story of the journey that he had taken, talking animatedly about it as he worked. On his map he drew, 'Gatwick airport', the 'mountains and sea' that he saw from the plane and several of the houses where he had stayed in India. Right at the end he drew over his drawing with black pencil because: 'It was night time when we came back.'

Several of the children were influenced by his talk of sea and beaches and began talking and drawing their own holidays.

The following day a small-world play scene was created on a table in the preschool room before the children arrived for the day. The route to the pet shop was marked out in grey paper, some small-world cars and people added, and a selection of pens was easily accessible so the children could add to the map if they wished. Many children began by playing with the cars and people inventing stories with them and each other, but then gradually they started drawing on the map.

One of the boys said he was drawing a pond between two roads and another child started to help him. Eventually his blue pen went onto a 'road'. This created great excitement and discussion as to what would happen to the cars.

The children and adults discussed how they could warn other drivers not to drive down the flooded road and three of the children decided to draw warning signs. One of the boys wrote 'ON' (NO). Another drew a circle with a line through it and then found some red paper and stuck it over the road. The third boy drew a T-shaped line by the side of the road. They all used their past experience and knowledge to solve the problem in different ways.

The careful documentation of 'making maps together' enabled the practitioner to discover how the different children in the group were developing their reasoning and thinking, and making sense of the world. By careful listening and timely intervention she was able to use the opportunity to move the children on to the next stage in their learning. The documentation was then shared with colleagues to help with the interpretation of what had happened. This, in turn, was later shared with the children's parents along with photographs taken and the actual maps which the children made.

Reference

Thornton, L. and Brunton, P. 'Treasureboxes', seminar at *Planning for Children's Learning – Making the Most of Emergent Objectives*. London, September 2004.

Further reading

Giudici, C., Rinaldi. C., and Krechevsky, M. (eds) (2001) *Making Learning Visible: Children as Individual and Group Learners*. Italy: Reggio Children.

This book looks at the learning of children and adults as individuals and in groups and gives an insight into the power of documentation.

Castagnetti, M. and Vecchi, V. (eds) (1997) *Shoe and Meter: Children and Measurement*. Italy: Reggio Children.

In the story told in this book, the children are confronted with a real-life situation. The school needs a new work table, one which will be identical to the others, the same size and the same shape. The children suggest that a carpenter is invited to preschool and asked to build the table. When the carpenter asks for the measurements the children agree to provide them. But then the challenge is set – 'Do you know how to measure?'

Trancossi, L. (ed.) (2001) *The Future is a Lovely Day.* Italy: Reggio Children.

From a project carried out in the Fiastri and Rodari preschools, a book that collects thoughts and predictions on the future by 5- and 6-year-old children.

'The future can only be seen in the witch's glass ball. We can't see it: I don't know if I'm going to be good tomorrow! To know that you have to study, to think with your head. The future is tomorrow 'cause the glass ball shows you what there'll be tomorrow or what there was before.'

Ferri, G. (ed.) (1999) *Everything has a Shadow Except Ants.* Italy: Reggio Children.

The children at the Diana and Gulliver preschools explore the everyday encounter with shadows. This book is built around their theories and thoughts about shadows and light.

Questions to think about

Developing children's ideas and theories

- Do we give children lots of opportunities to develop their ideas and knowledge about the world around them?
- Do we value asking questions, having conversations and listening to other points of view?
- How do we plan to ensure that we follow children's interests and build on what they already know?
- Is group learning valued in our setting?

Documenting children's learning

- How do the observation techniques and recording systems we currently use help us to focus closely on the process of learning?

- How closely do we pay attention to, and record, the detail of children's interactions, particularly with very young children?

- Do we capture the exact words the children use to describe their ideas and thoughts?

- In what ways can we help children to be actively involved in the documentation process?

Sharing children's learning

- Do we give children the opportunity to use documentation to revisit their ideas and develop their understanding?

- Could we make better use of documentation to help parents feel connected with their children's learning?

- Do we use documentation to celebrate children's learning within the local community?

- Do we keep evidence of past projects as part of the history of our setting?

7 | Reflective practice

In the Reggio Approach

The Charter of Rights

In 1993 Loris Malaguzzi proposed a Charter of Rights to define the rights of children, parents and teachers. The 'Rights of the Teacher' sets out what teachers are expected to do to contribute to the life of the schools, and what they can expect to receive in the way of support, help and guidance. All teachers contribute to the development of the educational philosophy and practice through discussion with colleagues, with the team of pedagogical advisers and with parents. In addition, they are required to cooperate in the organisation of the environment and resources and the daily organisation of the school. These expectations of individuals are supported by the 'flat' hierarchical management structure within the schools – everyone takes responsibility and plays their part.

Teachers as researchers

In Reggio it is felt that the role of the teacher is not only to teach, but also to learn. Staff take responsibility for their own professional development and learn from discussions and debates with colleagues, the atelieristas, the pedagogistas and with parents. There is an understanding that members of staff will constantly be improving their skills and knowledge and will be engaged in ongoing research into how young children learn.

Teachers work in pairs with a class group of children and regularly interact with one another throughout the working day. During the day there are timetabled opportunities for them to share observations with one another, look at documentation together and begin to interpret what they have seen. Reflecting on these observations and interpretations helps them to plan what opportunities and resources they will offer to the children the following day.

Weekly meetings involving the whole staff team, including the pedagogista and the atelierista, allow time for ideas and observations to be shared. Studying documentation of children's learning experiences at these meetings provides an opportunity to benefit from the viewpoints and past experiences of others. These weekly meetings are used as in-house staff training sessions for newer members of staff who then benefit in a very practical way from the experience of their colleagues. Everyone, regardless of experience, is expected to contribute their ideas and opinions at these meetings and all opinions are listened to, discussed and debated.

Revisiting documentation

The documentation which relates to projects which have been carried out some time in the past is kept within the schools and in a central archive known as the Documentation Centre. This information is a valuable record of children's learning and is frequently re-examined to provide information about the processes by which children learn. Documentation panels are retained in the preschools and infant-toddler centres and help to tell the story of the school. They remind children, parents and teachers of projects that have happened in the past. It is not unusual for teachers in Reggio to revisit a project which was carried out some years ago in order to see how a different group of children and adults respond to the same stimulus or starting point.

In the words of Carlina Rinaldi, pedagogical consultant to the Reggio Children organisation:

Documentation is not a technique, it is a way of guaranteeing that we are always reflective and valuing the other point of view. Documentation is a dialogue of the children's learning and our own development and knowledge.

(Rinaldi 2002)

Ongoing research

The Reggio Approach is itself a long-term educational research project which is constantly evolving. As educators learn more about how young children learn – through observation, interpretation, research and reflection – they change and adapt the way they work.

Research is a normal part of daily life in the infant-toddler centres and preschools, and not something reserved only for academics and universities. Large-scale research projects have been carried out on the relationship between the physical environment of the buildings and the educational philosophy and practice, involving children, parents, teachers, architects and designers. The findings from this research then influence the layout and design of the spaces for children, teachers and parents (*see* Chapter 4).

Recently educators in Reggio have been involved in research on two key areas of their buildings – bathrooms and entrances. They looked at the purpose of these spaces, how they were used, how attractive they were and how they could be improved. One very practical outcome of this research was to move water play into the bathroom area. This attention to detail is typical of the way in which all aspects of the Reggio Approach are constantly being reviewed to understand better how they contribute to the learning and development of babies and young children.

International networks

Worldwide interest in the early childhood services of Reggio Emilia has led to the creation of an international network of educators inspired by the Reggio Approach. The Wonder of Learning – The Hundred Languages of Children exhibition displays the documentation of some of the long-term projects carried out in the preschools and infant-toddler centres. This exhibition tours the world and has brought a taste of the Reggio Approach to many hundreds of thousands of educators and parents. Study groups from all over the world visit Reggio Emilia every year to visit the schools and hear about their work. In February 2006 the Loris Malaguzzi International Centre was opened in Reggio Emilia to act as a base for study visits, international studentships and ongoing research.

Reflective practice in the Early Years Foundation Stage

All providers should continuously think about how to improve what they are offering to children and families. Effective practitioners use their own learning to improve their work with young children in ways that are sensitive, positive and non-judgemental.

They are expected to develop, demonstrate and continuously improve their:

- relationships with both children and adults;
- understanding of the individual and the diverse ways in which children learn and develop;
- knowledge and understanding in order to actively support and extend children's learning in and across all areas and aspects of learning;
- practice in meeting all children's needs, learning styles and interests;
- work with parents, carers and the wider community;
- work with other professionals within and beyond the setting.

A high-quality, continuously improving setting will provide:

- well qualified and experienced staff who have access to opportunities for continuous professional development at all levels;

- opportunities to share best practice between early years settings;
- an environment that recognises the impact of higher qualifications on the quality of provision.

Inspiration from Reggio

Working as part of a team

Valuing each other's expertise and experience, and being happy to learn from one another, provides an ideal role model for children to follow. They will see clearly how much mutual respect there is between members of the staff team and will understand how different people can take the lead at different times depending on the nature of the activity. Sharing observations, listening carefully to what your colleagues have to

Adults sharing creative talents and skills enhance the learning
of children and adults

say and valuing their opinions will all help to create a culture of reflective practice in your setting.

Supporting young children's learning and development by finding different ways of encouraging their creative expression is fundamental to the way teachers in Reggio work. To do this they bring their own interests, skills and experience to the work that they do. All of us have interests and talents which, with a little thought, can add to the quality and breadth of the experiences we provide for children. These interests may be in art, science, music, dance, photography, environmental awareness, cooking, sewing, weaving, woodwork or gardening. All of these provide wonderful starting points for projects and experiences from which children can learn.

Welcoming adults with particular creative skills into your setting to work alongside you and the children will enhance the learning experience for everyone. Actors, architects, dancers, designers, engineers, musicians, painters, photographers, sculptors all have skills and talents you can draw on to enhance young children's learning. Not only do

Time for sharing, listening, discussion and planning

these individuals bring particular skills to share with children and staff, they also bring their different ways of looking at the world. To make the most of these opportunities it is essential to spend time planning in advance. It needs to be clear to everyone that the purpose is to provide starting points for discussions with the children and then to follow their ideas. The adults have skills and expertise to share but do not have total control over the outcome of the project. In this way everyone – adults and children – learns from one another.

The staff team as a learning group

Being a reflective practitioner is challenging as it involves constant ques-tioning, of oneself, and by colleagues, of what has happened in the past and what has been learned from it. To do this successfully we have to accept the value of constructive comment, not as criticism, but as a way to improve what we do in the future. As a society we tend to find this difficult and it is certainly an area which any staff team needs to work on over time in order to create the atmosphere of trust and support that is needed.

Effective reflective practice requires regular staff meetings at which documentation, observations and interpretations are shared and discussed. These are opportunities for staff members working with one age group to share observations and ideas with others responsible for older or younger children. Sharing experiences in this way adds value to the interpretations already made and throws up new ideas and questions to be pursued. Over time the staff team adds significantly to its collective body of knowledge about how babies and young children learn, all of which will inform and improve future practice (*see* Chapter 6).

Action research

Action research, involving practitioners working directly with children, is similar to the style of educational research which underpins the Reggio Approach. An action research project is an ideal way to develop the cycle of planning, doing and observing, reflecting and then making new plans on the basis of what has been learned. Action research projects work best if they are small-scale and focused enough to be manageable, and result in some change in practice at the end. By their very nature they involve colleagues and children, and often parents, so they are an ideal way to promote collaboration and team working.

As an action research project you may decide to look at how one particular area of your setting, for example the role-play area, is used by the children and staff. Over the course of a week you may plan to make regular observations of the use of the area to answer the following questions:

- Who uses the area – boys or girls?

- How big are the groups?

- What sorts of imaginative play and conversations go on there?

- How do children access the resources they need?

- Do adults become involved in activities happening in the area?

Ideally these observations would be collected by more than one member of staff, to gain different viewpoints on what is happening. At the end of the week the observations are collated and shared with other members of the staff team. You may also want to share your observations with the children so they can make their comments.

Reflecting together on what you have seen will help you to interpret your observations and draw some conclusions. Inevitably many more questions will arise which will help you to plan your next piece of action research. You may then decide to:

- change the way the area is resourced – perhaps by substituting more open-ended resources such as hats, bags, fabric and shoes, rather than specific 'dressing-up' costumes;

- plan to change the theme monthly to create the basics for a garage, a museum, a recording studio or a building site, for example;

- agree on a strategy to enable adults to be available to facilitate children's play, if invited.

Professional development networks

Supporting a research-based approach to children's learning and development in your setting is not something which can be done in isolation. Remember, in Reggio, teachers have the advantage of being part of a network of preschools and infant-toddler centres which all subscribe to the same philosophy and support one another. Becoming a member of a professional development network will enable you to share your ideas with a wider audience, learn from the experiences of others and tap in to a wide range of help and support.

Snapshot

The following snapshot illustrates how children's learning was enhanced through an action research project involving a staff team, an early years advisory team, parents and children collaborating together.

Treasureboxes®

For some time staff in a nursery had been thinking about how they could improve the way in which they communicated with parents about the importance of young children's play in the Early Years Foundation Stage. In particular they wanted to encourage parents to become active participants in their children's learning.

Following a discussion between the early years advisory team and the setting staff, it was agreed that they would develop a small library of interesting and unusual resources to share with families. The staff team then participated in training on Treasureboxes® – collections of interesting and unusual resources to promote exploration and investigation. Following the training session the staff decided to use the idea of Treasurebox collections on the theme of light, to share with families.

Weekly workshops were set up at which parents, practitioners and children met together to choose a range of resources to include in a Treasurebox collection to take home. These selections were based on practitioners' previous observations of the sorts of resources and ideas which the child might be interested in. Also included in the box were a disposable camera and a notepad for parents to use to record their observations. Families borrowed the Treasurebox for approximately a week and were asked to observe and note what their child did with the resources at home. When the Treasurebox was returned the practitioner spent time talking with the families about their observations on how the resources had been used.

The ideas developed by children at home were then shared with the rest of the child's group and used as the starting point for new explorations and investigations in the nursery.

Sharing information in this way, and basing future planning in the nursery around ideas and activities carried out at home, gave parents and children a very powerful message about the importance of including family members in supporting and extending young children's learning.

Reference

Rinaldi, C. 'Teachers as Researchers' Presentation at *ReFocus One Symposium*. Kendal, UK, June 2002.

Further reading

Giudici, C., Rinaldi. C., and Krechevsky, M. (eds) (2001) *Making Learning Visible: Children as Individual and Group Learners*. Italy: Reggio Children.

A joint publication with Project Zero at Harvard University in America. This looks at the learning of children and adults in groups and gives very detailed examples of daily life in a preschool and infant-toddler centre. It is an ideal text for supporting continuous professional development.

Questions to think about

Working as part of a team

- How well do we each contribute to the staff team?
- How do we value the contributions of others?
- Do we make time to share and discuss observations?
- Is best use made of everybody's creative skills and talents?

Creating a learning group

- Do we view ourselves as active learners?
- Is ongoing professional development part of the culture of our setting?
- How good is our structure for feeding back information from training to the rest of the team?
- Can we create a space for study, discussion and research?

Action research and networking

- How can we fit action research into our daily practice?
- Have we created the link between action research and quality improvement?
- Do we value time for professional networking?
- Are we confident to share our observations with others outside our setting?

Conclusion

This brief description of the Reggio Approach to early childhood, and how it has influenced early years practice in the UK, shows how many values and principles we have in common.

There are clear differences between the United Kingdom and Reggio Emilia in northern Italy. Our early childhood services have been developed against a different historic, cultural, geographic, political and economic background.

Nevertheless, we hold the same key principles of quality in early years practice:

- having clear values and a vision to which everyone subscribes;
- actively listening to children and respecting their ideas;
- fostering children's creativity;
- giving time to build on what children already know and what interests them;
- creating an effective and attractive environment for learning and development;
- valuing the contribution of parents, carers and families.

The key to improving quality in early years settings is to develop reflective practice among all practitioners. Understanding more about the Reggio Approach will help you to develop high-quality practice which is appropriate to your own culture and context. While taking inspiration from the work of the educators in Reggio Emilia, it is important not to lose sight of the rich history and traditions found in the best early childhood settings in the United Kingdom.

In the words of Aldo Fortunati of the University of Bologna:

Trust in the richness of your own context.

(Crossing Boundaries International Conference,
February 2004, Reggio Emilia)

Useful contacts

Reggio Children

Reggio Children is the organisation that represents the preschools and infant-toddler centres of Reggio Emilia. It provides information on the Reggio Approach, produces books and newsletters and organises international study visits. *ReChild*, the Reggio Children newsletter, is downloadable from the Reggio Children website at the following address: www.reggiochildren.it/?lang=en

Sightlines Initiative

Sightlines is the UK reference point for Reggio Children. It organises study tours to visit the preschools and infant-toddler centres in Reggio and runs Re Focus, a regional professional development network. It has an online bookshop where the publications mentioned in this book can be purchased. More information is available on the Sightlines website, www.sightlines-initiative.com

Reflections on Learning

Reflections on Learning produce a range of open-ended resources including light boxes and mirror resources inspired by the Reggio

Approach. The full range of products can be viewed on their website, www.reflectionsonlearning.co.uk

Reflections Nursery

Reflections Nursery in Worthing draws its inspiration from the practice of the preschools and infant-toddler centre of Reggio Emilia. Established in 2006 it now has many years worth of documentation of children's projects, some of which has been published in book form. The nursery runs regular professional development days to share ideas and reflective practice with like-minded colleagues. More information can be found on their website, www.reflectionsnurseries.co.uk